1001 PITFALLS IN *German*

Second Edition

Henry Strutz
**Formerly Associate Professor of Languages
SUNY Agricultural and Technical College
at Alfred, New York**

**Barron's Educational Series, Inc.
New York/ London/ Toronto/ Sydney**

All inquiries should be addressed to:
Barron's Educational Series, Inc.
250 Wireless Boulevard
Hauppauge, New York 11788

Library of Congress Catalog Card No. 86-17403

International Standard Book No. 0-8120-3718-9

Library of Congress Cataloging in Publication Data
Strutz, Henry.
   1001 pitfalls in German.

   Bibliography: p. 210
   Includes index.
   Summary: A supplementary textbook outlining fundamentals of the
German language and providing help for common obstacles such as
declensions, pronoun agreement, time expressions, and letter writing.
   1. German language—Text-books for foreign speakers—
English. 2. German language—Errors of usage.
3. German language—Grammar—1950-   . [1. German
language—Grammar] I. Title. II. Title: One thousand one
pitfalls in German.

PF3129. E5S77   1986   438.2'421   86-17403
ISBN 0-8120-3718-9

PRINTED IN THE UNITED STATES OF AMERICA

0123   800   98765

Contents

■ Preface

In language study, as in other disciplines, the complex is based on mastery of the simple. It may be possible to read English or history assignments just before an exam but this approach does not work well in language courses. Therefore, you should not hesitate to ask your teacher, from the very beginning, if anything is unclear to you, even in simple sentences such as *Mutter ist hier* or *Das Gras ist grün*. You should also, of course, do all the exercises assigned, on a daily basis. When these exercises are corrected, do not hesitate to ask questions. Your teacher will be pleased that you are sufficiently concerned to ask. This willingness to ask questions is particularly important for beginning students but also applies to those on the intermediate and advanced levels.

This second edition of *1001 Pitfalls in German* has been completely redesigned to make it easier to use. Rules and pitfalls of German grammar have been highlighted throughout the text to help you find the information you need. The book is divided into three major sections: Parts of Speech; Sentence Structure; and lastly, Special Aids. You will find a bibliography at the end to guide you in further readings.

One difficulty in the study of German, and other subjects, is that students often fail to see language in the context of life. Most teachers seek to impart a knowledge of the structural features of the language so that students can use the language, so that it can be a source of pleasure and inspiration to them. Many topics in this book are cross-listed. For example, the old-fashioned Saxon genitive could have been listed with nouns or articles. But since the pitfall lies in its use with prepositions, it is discussed there. Similarly, the extended adjective construction could have been discussed with adjectives or verbs (participles). But it is found in the chapter, "Word Order and Sentence Structure," since student problems center around word order when this construction is encountered. Grammars, and this book, break down and analyze the parts only in order to enable you to better understand the whole. The parts of speech form an organic unity, and you should strive to synthesize after achieving clear and distinct ideas of the parts.

Bringing as many of the senses as possible to the learning process facilitates that process. A variety of recent experiments confirms that the combination of words and music fix language patterns better in the mind. Many songs are an important and integral part of the German tradition. Familiarity with them will help you not only to understand the German language, but also the Germans better. Even if you don't live in a city like New York with its many fine FM stations that frequently play a wealth of German music (popular, folk, lieder, opera) you can listen to records. You may not understand everything being sung, but some things will stick. For beginners, even popular songs with their *Herz/Schmerz, Liebe/Triebe* rhymes (comparable to all the "moon/June," "far apart/in my heart," "charms/arms" rhymes in English), will be of value, and besides enriching vocabulary, they will impart a feeling for the rhythm of the language. Sociologists and historians will find many German cabaret songs (Brecht, Ringelnatz, Kästner and Tucholsky, etc.) of interest. Others will derive pleasure and linguistic profit from Wagner, Weber, Schubert, and many others. If you are religious, there are the many cantatas of Bach and others. On a more mundane level, *Blasmusik,* or "oom-pah-pah," and waltz and operetta tunes, have a wide appeal. There are also thousands of German drinking songs. It is not enough to hear a few songs occasionally in the language lab. Get records, turn on the radio, and start listening attentively. If possible, get the printed texts which often accompany record albums.

German-speaking individuals have made many outstanding contributions in a variety of fields. If you have a specialized interest in history, psychology, theology, literary and artistic movements such as Expressionism, or in many scientific disciplines, this should be of help. The best motivation for studying German is love for the language as a vehicle of the human spirit. Language is perhaps the noblest form of human expression, as many philosophers, Descartes for instance, have long maintained.

What happens outside the classroom is crucial. Language learning cannot be relegated to 50 minutes a few times a week. You didn't learn your own language that way. Language is intimately connected with life and the learning of language should be interrelated and integrated with as many aspects of life as possible. Everyone can listen to music, eat Wiener Schnitzel or Sachertorte, and quaff Münchner Löwenbräu or Henkell Trocken champagne. The more German you know, the better they'll taste. Learning a language is a matter of exposure and practice.

This book concerns itself with pitfalls. Pitfall means hidden danger and can have a sinister, military connotation. Perhaps you are in a state of war with German grammar and have fallen upon many minefields and into many pits. The whole German language may seem like one great bog to you. Sentences that seem to stretch on to infinity, verbs piled up at the end, compound nouns and compound numbers, all make for compound confusion. Before you can climb out of the pits and scale the heights of Goethe, Nietzsche, Rilke, Freud, etc., you must be able to recognize the basic structural features of German. This book aims to introduce peace and harmony where there were strife and discord. If possible pitfalls are pointed out, you can be made aware of them and thus learn to avoid them. Differences from English, especially where English might mislead you, are pointed out frequently. Traditional grammar terms are used throughout this book. In a few instances, modern terminology is mentioned.

This book is both a reference work and supplementary text suitable for use on all levels. Although many fine points of German grammar have been covered, much attention has been paid to fundamentals. The book should therefore be of considerable use to beginning students in both high school and college. Grammar topics such as declensions and conjugations have been treated not merely in terms of the pitfalls possible in connection with their use but have also been discussed as such, sometimes in detail.

Learning a language is a great adventure. It should be filled more with pleasure than with pitfalls. It is hoped that this book will reduce the dangers and thus increase the pleasure.

Henry Strutz

PARTS OF SPEECH

1 ■ Adjectives and Adverbs

ADJECTIVES

Descriptive **adjectives** describe or identify a person or thing (beautiful—*schön*, rich—*reich*, green—*grün*, etc.). The limiting adjectives, or *der-* and *ein-* words are discussed in the chapter "Cases, Articles, Der- and Ein- Words."

Adjectives Without Endings

Declining adjectives in German is troublesome. Perhaps you would agree with the American student at Heidelberg who allegedly told Mark Twain that he would rather "decline two drinks than one German adjective."

RULE

Predicate adjectives that complete the verbs *bleiben, sein,* and *werden* come after the noun they modify and have no ending.

Der Polizist war sehr höflich.
The police officer was very polite.

Sein Bruder wurde sehr reich.
His brother became very rich.

Das Wetter bleibt schön.
The weather remains good.

You will also occasionally come across literary or proverbial and idiomatic uses of adjectives without endings.

Kinder, groß und klein, spielten im Hof.
Children, big and small, were playing in the yard.

ein politisch Lied, ein garstig Lied (Goethe)
a political song, an ugly song

Es reifet euch ein schrecklich Ende (Bach, *Cantata #90*)
A terrible end is looming for you

bin doch ein arm einfältig Mann (Hans Sachs in Wagner's *Die Meistersinger*)
I'm just a poor, simple fellow

Es ist ein mächtig Ding das Gold (Rocco in Beethoven's *Fidelio*)
Gold is a mighty thing

Adjective Endings

> **RULE**
>
> Except for the literary and idiomatic uses just noted, German adjectives which precede the nouns they modify (attributive adjectives) have endings.

STRONG ENDINGS

> **RULE**
>
> If no *der-* or *ein-* word (limiting adjective) precedes the adjective, the adjective endings indicate case, hence the name "strong." The strong endings resemble the endings of *der, die, das* and the *der* words (*dieser,* etc.) except in the genitive singular masculine and neuter where *-en* instead of *-es* occurs.

	USES OF STRONG ENDINGS		
	Masc.	**Fem.**	**Neuter**
Nom.	*guter* Wein	*gute* Suppe	*gutes* Bier
Gen.	*guten* Weines	*guter* Suppe	*guten* Bieres
Dat.	*gutem* Wein	*guter* Suppe	*gutem* Bier
Acc.	*guten* Wein	*gute* Suppe	*gutes* Bier

Plural (all genders)

Nom.	*gute* Weine (Suppen, Biere)
Gen.	*guter* Weine (Suppen, Biere)
Dat.	*guten* Weinen (Suppen, Bieren)
Acc.	*gute* Weine (Suppen, Biere)

---

1. After cardinal numbers, adjectives have strong endings.

drei rote Rosen
three red roses

zwei schöne grüne Äpfel
two nice green apples

2. Strong adjectives can be used with expletive force.

Herrliches Wetter, was?
Beautiful weather, isn't it?

Leuchtende Liebe, lachender Tod! (Wagner's *Siegfried*)
Gleaming love, laughing death!

Höchste Lust! (Wagner's *Tristan und Isolde*)
Highest bliss!

3. Strong endings are used on "dear" in the salutation of letters, since no *der-* or *ein-* word precedes, as a rule. (See Letter Writing, p. 165)

Lieber Freund! Liebe Freundin!
Dear Friend,

Liebes Kind!
Dear Child,

Sehr geehrte Herren!
Dear Sirs:

4. The strong adjective endings indicate case. They have *der-* word endings except in the masculine and neuter genitive singular where the *-s* or *-es* ending on the noun does this "case work." Contrast:

Er mag starken Kaffee. (Accusative)
He loves strong coffee.

Er mag das Aroma starken Kaffees. (Genitive)
He loves the aroma of strong coffee.

WEAK ENDINGS

> **RULE**
>
> The weak endings are used on adjectives following a *der-* word. There are only two, *-e* or *-en*. All three genders have *-e* in the nominative singular; *-e* is also the ending in the feminine and neuter accusative. In all other cases, the adjective ends in *-en*.

	Masc.	Fem.	Neuter
Nom.	der blaue	die schwarze	das kalte
	Engel	Spinne	Herz
Gen.	des blauen	der schwarzen	des kalten
	Engels	Spinne	Herzens
Dat.	dem blauen	der schwarzen	dem kalten
	Engel	Spinne	Herzen
Acc.	den blauen	die schwarze	das kalte
	Engel	Spinne	Herz

In the plural, all four cases have the ending *-en*.

MIXED ENDINGS

> **RULE**
>
> Adjectives following an *ein-* word take the mixed endings.

This declension is called mixed because in the three forms (nom. sing. masc., and nom. and accus. neuter) where *ein-* words have no ending and thus do not indicate the case, a strong ending is used. The adjective endings *-e* and *-en* are weak. The endings *-er* and *-es* are strong, i.e., they indicate case where the *ein-* word does not.

ADJECTIVES IN SERIES

> **RULE**
>
> All adjectives preceding the same noun have the same ending.

das junge, gesunde, schöne Mädchen
the young, healthy, beautiful girl
ein junges, gesundes, schönes Mädchen
a young, healthy, beautiful girl
das große, heilige Köln (Heine)
great, holy Cologne

FOREIGN ADJECTIVE ENDINGS

> **RULE**
>
> Foreign adjectives ending in -*a* are not declined.

ein rosa Kleid   rosa Kleider
a pink dress   pink dresses
prima Qualität
first quality

Some Germans are unsure of these. If the adjective refers to a color, they add -*farben* which is then declined like any other adjective.

ein rosafarbenes Kleid   rosafarbene Kleider
a pink dress   pink dresses

ADJECTIVES WITH A FINAL -E

> **RULE**
>
> A few adjectives may be written either with or without a final -*e*. It is not an adjective ending and makes no difference as far as inflection is concerned.

blöd(e) (dopey, stupid)
bös(e) (mean, angry, bad)
fad(e) (insipid; trite)
feig(e) (cowardly)
irr(e) (confused)
leis(e) (gentle, soft)

mild(e) (mild, gentle)
müd(e) (tired)
öd(e) (desolate)
träg(e) (sluggish, lazy)
trüb(e) (troubled, cloudy)
vag(e) (vague)
zäh(e) (tough)

One may say either:

Der Mann ist müde.

or

Der Mann ist müd.

Both mean, "The man is tired." This optional -*e* has no effect on adjective endings.

der müde Mann   ein müder Mann
the tired man   a tired man

PITFALL

Many adjectives take the dative. They usually correspond to "to" in English, but *für-* NOT *zu-* constructions can sometimes be substituted.

nützlich (useful)   (un)angenehm ((un)pleasant)
lästig (burdensome)   schädlich (harmful)
. wichtig (important)   (un)begreiflich ((in)compre-
leicht (easy)   hensible)
(un)möglich ((im)possible)   unzulänglich (insufficient)
unentbehrlich (indispensable)

Unlike English, German adjectives with the dative usually follow the dative noun or pronoun dependent on them. The *für* construction usually precedes.

Dieses Buch war ihr sehr nützlich.
This book was very useful to her.

Dieses Buch war für sie sehr nützlich.
This book was very useful for her.

Seine Gegenwart ist mir lästig.
His presence is troublesome to me.

Seine Gegenwart ist für mich lästig.
His presence is troublesome to (for) me.

Das Medikament wurde seiner Tante unentbehrlich.
The medication became indispensable to his aunt.

Das Medikament wurde für seine Tante unentbehrlich.
The medication became indispensable to his aunt.

Ihm war es leicht.
It was easy for him.

Für ihn war es leicht.
It was easy for him.

RULE

Do not use forms of *ein* to translate "one" in the following examples. German merely omits the noun.

„Wollen Sie das grüne oder das rote Kleid?" „Das grüne."
"Do you want the green or the red dress?" "The green one."

„Haben Sie das alte oder das neue Haus gekauft?" „Das alte."
"Did you buy the old or the new house?" "The old one."

So glaube jeder sicher seinen Ring den echten. (Lessing)
Let each one believe firmly that his ring is the genuine one.

Adjectival Nouns

RULE

German makes far more extensive use of adjectives as nouns than does English. Remember to capitalize *all* nouns and to maintain the same ending on an adjectival noun that it would have had if the noun were still present to indicate gender, case and number.

Wenn das Haus eines Großen zusammenbricht
werden viele Kleine erschlagen (Brecht)
When a great man's house collapses
Many little people are destroyed

To help you to understand adjectival nouns you should, if necessary, mentally supply or write out the noun, for example, *eines großen Mannes* and *viele kleine Leute* in the example just given. C. F. Meyer and Theodor Storm are two famous 19th-century poets. Each one has a poem called *Einer Toten*. Because of the case ending *-er*, Germans know that the title means "To A Dead Woman," and not "To A Dead Man" (*Einem Toten*).

Die Toten is an adjectival noun meaning, "the dead." The *Totentanz*, a popular theme in European art, literature, and music, is usually translated "Dance of Death," which in German would be *Todestanz*. "Dance of the Dead" would be a more precise translation for *Totentanz*.

You will often encounter adjectival nouns in titles of books or operas:

> *Der Erwählte* (Thomas Mann)
>
> *Die Kluge* (Carl Orff)
>
> *Der Schwierige* (Hugo von Hofmannsthal)

If these works had been written about more than one "chosen," "clever," or "difficult" individual, the article would have been *die* and then in each case the adjective would end in *-en* (*Die Erwählten, Die Klugen, Die Schwierigen*).

PITFALL

Do not capitalize adjectives derived from names of countries or geographical regions.

ein französischer Wein
a French wine
ein spanischer Tanz
a Spanish dance
ein deutsches Bier
a German beer

Wir tranken zuerst einen russischen, dann einen polnischen Wodka.
First we drank a Russian, then a Polish Vodka.

Essen Sie lieber iranischen oder russischen Kaviar?
Do you prefer Iranian or Russian caviar?

RULE

Abstract nouns formed from adjectives are neuter.

Wenn das Anständige dem Gemeinen begegnet, verliert das Anständige. (W. Weyrauch)
When the decent meets the base, the decent loses.

Er schrieb eine Arbeit über das Gute, Wahre, und Schöne bei Schiller.
He wrote on the true, good, and beautiful in Schiller's works.

Such use of abstract, adjectival nouns sometimes has to be translated freely as "that which is." Sometimes "thing" is inserted.

Das Beste daran war das Geld, das ich dafür bekommen habe.
The best thing about it was the money I got for it. (Wagner's reference to a march he wrote for the celebration of America's Centennial in 1876.)

English uses adjectival nouns chiefly in a few plurals. When rendering them in German it is, of course, necessary to use the plural.

Die Reichen werden reicher und die Armen ärmer.
The rich get richer and the poor get poorer.

Die Guten sterben jung.
The good die young.

RULE

In English one says "the good" or "the old" in reference to people, while German says *die Guten, die Alten.* When referring to an abstract concept German uses a neuter.

---

das Alte (that which is old, old things)
das Gute (that which is good)

PITFALL

The adjectives *hell* means "light" only in the sense opposed to "dark." "Difficult" or "heavy" in German is *schwer.* Its opposite, "easy" is *leicht.* The noun "the light" is *das Licht.* Do not confuse *hell* "light" with English "hell" which in German is *die Hölle.* (For similar confusions see the list in Chapter 12, p. 197.)

Sie trug ein helles Kleid.
She wore a light (colored) dress.

Der helle Anzug wird zu schnell schmutzig.
The light suit gets dirty too fast.

The story is told of a Viennese dressmaker in New York who told a customer to "go to hell." What she wanted to say was, *Gehen Sie ins Helle, bitte!* or "Move toward the light, please."

Comparison of Adjectives and Adverbs

RULE

In English, adjectives and adverbs are compared in two ways. Monosyllables add *-er* in the comparative and *-est* in the superlative. Polysyllabic adjectives use "more" and "most." German uses only the *-er* comparative and *-(e)st* superlative. Do not use *mehr* and *meist* to translate "more" and "most" when comparing adjectives and adverbs.

Helene kleidet sich eleganter als Gertrud.
Helene dresses more elegantly than Gertrud.

Hans ist intelligenter als Georg.
Hans is more intelligent than Georg.

Der Zug ist schneller als der Bus.   .
The train is faster than the bus.   .

Note: Mehr or preferably *eher* may be used when comparing two different qualities.

Er ist mehr (eher) dumm als böse.
He is more stupid than evil.

Most one-syllable adjectives with *a, o,* and *u* add an umlaut in the comparative and superlative forms.

stark, stärker, am stärksten (der, die, das stärkste)
grob, gröber, am gröbsten (der, die, das gröbste)
dumm, dümmer, am dümmsten (der, die, das dümmste)

Exception: klar, klarer, am klarsten (der, die, das klarste)

PITFALL

No umlaut is ever added for the comparative and superlative forms of adjectives with *au.*

laut, lauter, am lautesten (der, die, das lauteste)
vertraut, vertrauter, am vertrautesten (der, die, das vertrauteste)

RULE

Adjectives ending in -*d,* -*t,* -*tz,* -*s,* -*ß,* -st, or *z* add -*est,* not -*st,* to form the superlative.

Exceptions to this rule are adjectives ending in -*isch,* present participles (all end in -*d*) used as adjectives, and the adjective *groß.*

das süßeste Mädchen
the sweetest girl

die breiteste Straße
the widest street

But:

der launischste Mensch
the moodiest person

das blühendste Geschäft
the most flourishing business

die größte Blume
the biggest flower

PITFALL

It is far more idiomatic and common in German to use *immer* plus the comparative to express the English double comparative (smaller and smaller, faster and faster, etc.).

Sie wurde immer dicker.
She got fatter and fatter.

Immer leiser wird mein Schlummer.
My slumber grows ever more gentle.

Er ging immer schneller.
He walked faster and faster.

PITFALL

Adjectives add -*er* in the comparatives. This -*er* should not be confused with the adjective ending -*er*. Adjectives in the comparative are treated like all other adjectives and can take strong, weak, or mixed endings when they precede a noun.

Positive	*Comparative*
ein feiner Wein	ein feinerer Wein
a fine wine	a finer wine
ein schöner Traum	ein schönerer Traum
a beautiful dream	a more beautiful dream

False Comparative

RULE

The comparative form may express a true comparison or may be a "false" or "absolute" comparative.

The false or absolute comparative is often translated by "rather" or "fairly" and indicates a fair or extensive amount of the quality involved. This is an idiomatic usage.

Er hat eine größere Wohnung.
He has a rather large apartment.

Hameln ist eine kleinere Stadt.
Hameln is a fairly small town.

Paradoxically, *eine ältere Dame* "an elderly lady" is younger than *eine alte Dame* "an old lady," and *eine größere Wohnung* "a fairly large apartment" is smaller than *eine große Wohnung*. Similarly, *eine höhere Schule* is not as academically elevated as a *Hochschule*.

Comparisons of Equality and Inequality

RULE

In the meaning "than" use *als* in comparisons of inequality (superiority or inferiority). Use *wie* "as" for comparisons of equality.

Since *als* and *wie* can both mean "as," they are very often confused, even by Germans.

Comparisons of Inequality

Fritz ist zwei Jahre älter als ich.
Fritz is two years older than I.

Inge ist schöner als Luise.
Inge is more beautiful than Luise.

Max ist dümmer als Otto.
Max is dumber than Otto.

Der Bus ist langsamer als der Zug.
The bus is slower than the train.

Comparisons of Equality

Fritz ist so alt wie ich.
Fritz is as old as I am.

Inge ist so schön wie Luise.
Inge is as beautiful as Luise.

Er ist so langweilig wie sein Vater.
He's as boring as his father.

PITFALL

Use *als* for English "than" as in the above examples of unequal comparison, not *dann* or *denn*. *Dann* is used to express "then" in time sequences.

Und dann habe ich gefrühstückt.
And then I ate breakfast.

Dann sind wir fortgegangen.
Then we went away.

Note: In older German, *denn* was used synonymously for *als*. This survives today only in set phrases like *mehr denn je* "more than ever." It can also be used to avoid a repetition of *als*:

Dieser Künstler wurde mehr als Bildhauer denn als Maler bekannt.
This artist became more famous as a sculptor than as a painter.

RULE

The superlative stem cannot stand by itself when used as a predicate adjective (one that comes after the noun it modifies) or as an adverb. In those instances it is preceded by *am* and ends in *-en*. Usually, if "the" is not expressed in English, the *am . . . -en* form is used.

Karl fährt am schnellsten.
Karl drives fastest.

Sie tanzt am besten.
She dances best.

Im Frühling ist das Wetter am angenehmsten.
In the spring the weather is (the) most pleasant.

Contrast the preceding with the following where English and German use a definite article (the).

Karl ist der schnellste Fahrer.
Karl is the fastest driver.

Sie ist die beste Tänzerin.
She is the best dancer.

das angenehmste Wetter
the most pleasant weather

Irregular Comparisons

The following adjectives and adverbs form their comparative and superlative irregularly. Some are similar to English where, for example, it is incorrect to say "good, gooder, goodest" or "much, mucher, muchest."

gut	besser	am besten (der, die, das beste)
good	better	best
viel	mehr	am meisten (der, die, das meiste)
much	more	most
hoch	höher	am höchsten (der, die, das höchste)
high	higher	highest
gern	lieber	am liebsten
gladly	more gladly	most gladly

Gern may be used with any verb to indicate that one likes or enjoys the action of that verb. *Lieber* and *am liebsten* express preference or "rather."

Sie spielt gern.
She likes to play.

Sie singt lieber.
She prefers to sing. *Or:* She would rather sing.

Sie tanzt am liebsten.
She prefers most to dance. *Or:* She likes dancing best of all.

Er trinkt Tee gern.
He likes to drink tea.

Er trinkt Wein lieber.
He'd rather drink wine.

Er trinkt Kaffee am liebsten.
He'd most rather drink coffee.

A similar construction exists with *gern haben* "to like."

Er hat Tee gern.
He likes tea.

Er hat Wein lieber.
He likes wine better.

Er hat Kaffee am liebsten.
He likes coffee best.

The German word *lieb-* is related to the archaic English word "lief" which means "dear, willing, glad." Phrases like "I would liefer do it now" sometimes still survive and resemble the German construction, *Ich würde es lieber jetzt tun*. A better translation of the German is, of course, "I'd rather do it now."

ADVERBS

Adverbs modify verbs or adjectives. Since they never have endings, they pose few problems.

RULE

In English many adverbs are formed by adding *-ly*. The German ending *-lich* is an adjective ending or suffix to which weak, strong, or mixed endings can be added as to any other adjective. It can also be used as an adverb, like all adjectives in German.

Adjective

Er ist ein abscheulicher Mensch.
He is a repulsive person.

Ich danke für die freundliche Aufnahme.
Thank you for the friendly reception.

Adverb

Er benahm sich ganz abscheulich.
He behaved quite abominably.

Man hat uns sehr freundlich behandelt.
They treated us very nicely.

Adverbs are compared similarly to adjectives, although an absolute superlative in *aufs . . . ste* or *-stens* exists in addition to the regular superlative in *am -sten*.

Wir haben ihn aufs wärmste (wärmstens) empfohlen.
We recommended him most warmly.

Correct English distinguishes between "good" (adjective) and "well" (adverb). German *gut*, like all adjectives, may be used as an adverb.

Er hat es gut gemacht.
He did it well.

Note: To refer to how someone feels, *wohl* is used.

Er fühlt sich heute nicht wohl.
He isn't feeling well today.

PITFALL

English "this" is not expressed by German *dies* but by *heute* in adverbial phrases like the following:

heute morgen	**heute abend**
this morning	this evening
heute nachmittag	**heute nacht**
this afternoon	tonight

The above nouns are not capitalized since they are used adverbially, not as nouns.

PITFALL

Der Morgen means "the morning." "Tomorrow" is *morgen* and is not capitalized. "Tomorrow morning" is not *morgen morgen* but *morgen früh.*

Position of Adverbs

PITFALL

German word order is the reverse of English in the following expressions:

noch einmal	**sieh mal**
once more	just see
noch nicht	**warte nur**
not yet	just wait
noch eine Weile	**Punkt acht Uhr**
a while longer	8 o'clock sharp

RULE

In English an adverb may come between subject and verb. This never can be done in German with common adverbs.

He never drinks alone.
Er trinkt nie allein.

She always dances with him.
Sie tanzt immer mit ihm.
They sometimes forget everything they've learned.
Sie vergessen manchmal alles, was sie gelernt haben.
We already know the answer.
Wir wissen schon die Antwort.

PITFALL

Although it is very common in English, some teachers still insist that splitting an infinitive is wrong. In German it cannot be done at all.

to better understand
besser zu verstehen
to more fully enjoy
vollkommener zu genießen

RULE

Unlike English, adverbs of time always come before adverbs of place.

Sie will jetzt nach Hause gehen.
She wants to go home now.
Wir wollen bald in die Stadt fahren.
We want to go downtown soon.

This rule is referred to in German as *Zeit vor Platz*.

PITFALL

The position of *nicht* is variable, depending on which element of the sentence one wishes to negate. If *nicht* negates a particular element, then *nicht* is placed immediately before it. If the whole clause is negated, as in the first of the following examples, *nicht* is placed at the end. In the second example, not the father but someone else gives the money. In the third example, the father does transfer money but to someone else, not to his son. In the last example, the implication is that the father does indeed give something to his son, but not money. To give further emphasis to this idea one could write:

Nicht das Geld gibt der Vater dem Sohn.

(For a discussion of the common German practice of beginning a sentence with elements other than the subject, see the chapter on word order and sentence structure, p. 147.)

1. **Der Vater gibt dem Sohn das Geld nicht.**
   The father doesn't give the son the money.

2. **Nicht der Vater gibt dem Sohn das Geld.**
   Not (the) father gives the son the money.

3. **Der Vater gibt nicht dem Sohn das Geld.**
   Not to the son does the father give the money.

4. **Der Vater gibt dem Sohn nicht das Geld.**
   The father doesn't give the son the money. *or*
   Not the money does the father give to the son.

When the whole clause is negated, *nicht* stands at the end of the clause.

Ich habe das Buch nicht.
I don't have the book.

But it regularly precedes the following:

1. infinitives and participles

   Ich werde das Buch nicht lesen.
   I won't read the book.
   Ich habe das Buch nicht gelesen.
   I haven't read the book.

2. predicate adjectives

   Das Buch ist nicht alt.
   The book is not old.

3. predicate nouns

   Er ist nicht Rechtsanwalt, sondern Arzt.
   He is not a lawyer but a doctor.

4.   adverbs

Er ist nicht hier.
He isn't here.

5.   prepositional phrases

Er ist nicht in der Schule.
He is not in school.

RULE

The adverbs *auch* or *immer* (sometimes both) may be used with interrogatives like *wer, was, wo, wie,* to intensify the meaning.

They are then translated by "whoever, whatever, wherever," etc., or sometimes by "no matter" but *not* by "also" and "always."

Was sie auch tut, ist es ihm nie recht.
Whatever (no matter what) she does, he's never satisfied.

Wo immer sie auch stecken . . .
Wherever (no matter where) they may be . . .

Wie schön sie auch ist, hat sie doch einen schlechten Charakter.
However (no matter how) beautiful she is, she nevertheless has a bad character.

2 ■ Cases, Articles, Der- and Ein- Words

EXPLANATION OF CASES

Speakers of English need concern themselves with cases only when dealing with pronouns, since only pronouns are inflected, i.e., have cases. In German, the concept of case is extremely important not only for pronouns but also for other parts of speech such as nouns and adjectives. Prepositions, too, take some case other than the nominative.

If you saw the German sentences:

1. **Den Hund beißt der Mann.**
2. **Den Mann beißt der Hund.**
3. **Die bräutliche Schwester befreite der Bruder.** (Wagner, *Die Walküre*)

you could easily confuse them. But if you are aware of the use of the cases you will be able to translate them correctly as:

1. The man bites the dog.
2. The dog bites the man.
3. The brother has freed his sister and bride.

The inscription on Olbrich's *Sezession* Building in Vienna reads:

Der Zeit ihre Kunst
Der Kunst ihre Freiheit

which translates as, "To each time its art. To (that) art, its freedom." If you didn't recognize the cases, you would flounder.

Keeping gender, number, and case straight is essential in German. There are three genders (masculine, feminine, and neuter), two numbers (singular and plural), and four cases (nominative, genitive, dative, and accusative). This can make for 16 possible pitfalls. The concept of case is of basic importance in German. Many pitfalls come from not understanding this concept. Cases exist in English but their use is limited to pronouns. Even here

21

many misuse the cases. "Just between you and I," and "a gift from Jane and I" are common mistakes. Some also have difficulty recognizing a direct object. One hears sentences like, "Would you care to join Mary and I for a drink?" and, "They let John and I do it."

Your study of German will be made easier if you are able to understand the structure of the following simple English sentences.

1. Subject (Nominative) Verb   Direct Object (Accusative)
   John   writes   a letter.

2. Subject   Verb   Indirect Object (Dative)   Direct Object
   John   writes   his mother   a letter.

3. Subject Verb   Possessive (Genitive) Indirect Object Direct Object
   John   writes   his mother's   friend   a letter.

The last sentence can perhaps be more easily analyzed if the genitive (possessive) is expressed, as is often done in English, by "of" (although in this sentence it is less colloquial than the form with an apostrophe). Similarly, "to" helps to indicate the dative (indirect object).

4. Subject   Verb   Direct Object Indirect Object Possessive
   John   writes   a letter   to the friend   of his mother.

Whether English uses "to" and "of" or not, the cases of friend and mother are still dative and genitive, respectively. These sentences in German are as follows:

	Nom.	Verb	Accusative		
1.	John	schreibt	einen Brief.		

	Nom.	Verb	Dative	Accusative	
2.	John	schreibt	seiner Mutter	einen Brief.	

	Nom.	Verb	Dative	Genitive	Accusative
3.	John	schreibt	dem Freund	seiner Mutter	einen Brief.

NOMINATIVE CASE

The nominative is the case you start with. It names the subject and, as in grammatical if sometimes stilted English, is used after the verb "to be." This latter usage is not "schoolmarmy" in German.

GENITIVE CASE

The **genitive** indicates possession (genesis, origin) and is also used abverbially, after certain verbs, adjectives, and prepositions.

DATIVE CASE

The **dative** is used for the indirect object, as a dative of advantage or disadvantage, instead of a possessive adjective with parts of the body, and after certain verbs, prepositions, and adjectives. The name *dative* comes from the Latin "to give." One gives or shows, explains, writes, etc., something (accusative) to somebody (dative).

ACCUSATIVE CASE

The **accusative** is the case of the direct object, and is also used after certain prepositions and measurements. The accusative indicates definite time and extension of time. If John kicks, accuses, kills, strangles, etc., Jack, then the doer of the action is John (subject or nominative), whereas the object, the receiver of the action, is Jack (accusative).

The many special uses of the cases will be discussed under verbs, prepositions, etc.

In German, the cases may be designated by Latinate names (**Nominativ, Genitiv, Dativ, Akkusativ**) similar to those used in English or by: *Werfall, Wesfall, Wemfall,* and *Wenfall*. They are also known as *1., 2., 3.,* and *4. Fall* (erster, zweiter, etc.). So that a *Fall* (case) does not become a *Falle* (trap) all forms of *der, die, das* must be memorized. Despite the 16 possible case forms, the many identical forms reduce the labor. It is essential to be aware of the cases, i.e., where they fall or occur, and how they are used in a sentence. Once you have mastered the concept of case you may feel like proudly quoting the famous Dada poem, "*Ich bin der große Der Die Das*." You will then be able to face a *Fall* (case) with pride and observe where and how it falls without pitfalling yourself.

It is traditional to list the nominative first, then the genitive, dative, and accusative. Because of the similarities between the nominative and accusative, and between the dative and genitive in certain forms, many modern texts prefer to list first the nominative, followed by the accusative, dative, and genitive. Beginning students who change textbooks in their second or third semester are sometimes confused by this juggling. It must be emphasized that no matter how you slice it, it's still the same thing.

ARTICLES

The definite article (the) is declined most often as follows:

	Masc.	Fem.	Neuter	Plural (all genders)
Nom.	der	die	das	die
Gen.	des	der	des	der
Dat.	dem	der	dem	den
Acc.	den	die	das	die

Some texts give the feminine first. Others, because of the similarities mentioned above, prefer to list them as follows:

	Masc.	Neuter	Fem.	Plural (all genders)
Nom.	der	das	die	die
Acc.	den	das	die	die
Dat.	dem	dem	der	den
Gen.	des	des	der	der

The little word "the" (the definite article) has, thus, 16 possibilities in German. Remember to learn the gender and the plural of a noun at the same time you learn the noun itself (see Nouns). The *-er* ending, for example, may be a nominative singular masculine, a genitive or dative singular feminine, or a genitive plural.

RULE

The definite article may be used as a demonstrative pronoun.

It can denote familiarity or often be slightly more emphatic than the personal pronoun, and thus be translated as "that one."

Hast du mit dem Mann gesprochen?
Did you talk with the man?

Von dem könntest du was lernen.
You could learn something from him.

Von dem will ich nichts wissen.
I don't want anything to do with him (that one).

Mit der kann man nicht reden.
There's no talking to her (that one).

PITFALL

Unlike English, the definite article can be used with proper names, especially if modified by an adjective.

Der kleine Kurt geht schon in die Schule.
Little Kurt goes to school already.

Die dicke Anna trinkt gerne ihren Schnaps.
Fat Anna likes her liquor.

PITFALL

The definite article is very frequently joined with a dative in German where English would use a genitive, a possessive adjective, or an accusative.

Er füllte mir das Glas.
He filled my glass.

Der Appetit ist uns vergangen.
We've lost our appetite.

Sie zog dem Betrunkenen die Schuhe aus.
She took the drunk's shoes off.

RULE

The definite article is used after most prepositions most of the time, but in a few prepositional phrases where English usually uses a definite or indefinite article, German uses no article.

bei Ausbruch des Koreakrieges
at the outbreak of the Korean War

ein Pianist mit französischem Namen
a pianist with a French name

nach langer Zeit
after a long time

auch bei bestem Willen
even with the best intentions

> **RULE**
>
> When speaking of things in general, and with abstract nouns, German usually uses the definite article while English does not.

Schiller's famous ode *An die Freude* (set to music by Beethoven in the last movement of his 9th Symphony) is translated simply as "Ode To Joy" since the author is talking about joy in general. Similarly, Schubert's famous song, *An die Musik* (text by Schober) means "To Music."

So ist das Leben.
That's life.

Die Liebe ist eine Himmelsmacht. (J. Strauß, *Der Zigeunerbaron*)
Love is a divine force.

Der Tod, das ist die kühle Nacht
Das Leben ist der schwüle Tag. (Heine)
Death, that is the cool night
Life is the sultry day.

Nichts ist so häßlich wie die Rache.
Nothing is as ugly as revenge.

Nur wer die Sehnsucht kennt . . . (Goethe)
Only he who knows what yearning is . . .

Wer die Schönheit angeschaut mit Augen . . . (Platen)
Whoever has beheld beauty with his eyes . . .

Es ist ein mächtig Ding das Gold. (Beethoven, *Fidelio*)
Money (gold) is a mighty thing.

PITFALL

When used in an indefinite or partial sense and after some prepositions, the article is omitted as in English.

Er braucht Schlaf.
He needs sleep.

Ich suche Arbeit.
I'm looking for work.

Diese Musik hat Leben.
This music has life.

| **Durch Geduld und Arbeitsamkeit kommt man zum Ziel.**
By patience and diligence one will reach the goal.

RULE

Many common nouns and phrases in German use the definite article where English does not.

In the following examples *im* represents a contraction of *in* + *dem*. (For a listing of contractions with prepositions, see the conclusion of the chapter on prepositions, p 81.)

im Bett (in bed)   im Kongreß (in congress)
im Gefängnis (in prison)   im Paradies (in paradise)
im Himmel (in heaven)   im Parlament (in parliament)
in der Hölle (in hell)   in der Schule (in school)
in der Kirche (in church)   in der Stadt (in town)

RULE

Schule and *Kirche* are always used with the article in German.

---

nach der Schule (Kirche)   vor der Schule (Kirche)
after school (church)   before school (church)

Er geht zur Schule (Kirche).
He's going to school (church).

Die Schule (Kirche) hat ihm nicht geholfen.
School (church) hasn't helped him.

RULE

The definite article is always used before *meist-*.

Die meisten Plätze sind schon ausverkauft.
Most seats have already been sold.

Das meiste Geld ist weg.
Most of the money is gone.

DER- WORDS

Words declined like (having the same endings as) *der, die, das* are called *der-* words or sometimes *dieser-* words. The most common are:

dieser (this)	**mancher** (many a)
jeder (each, every)	**solcher** (such)
jener (that)	**welcher** (which, what)

The endings on *der-* words are also called "strong" or "primary" endings in some texts. Since *der-* and *ein-* words occur before nouns, they are frequently called "limiting adjectives" because they limit the meaning of the noun which they precede.

RULE

Dieser is used in modern German for both "this" and "that."

Haben Sie diesen Baum gepflanzt?
Did you plant this (that) tree?

Ich kann diese Musik nicht leiden.
I can't stand this (that) music.

If German wishes to emphasize distance from the speaker, *da* or *dort drüben* is used.

Haben Sie den Baum da gepflanzt?
Did you plant that tree (there)?

Sehen Sie die Frau dort drüben?
Do you see that lady over there?

Jener (English cognate "yonder") is somewhat stilted and is used chiefly to distinguish between two possibilities.

Dieser Baum ist tot, aber jener lebt noch.
This tree is dead but that one is still alive.

·PITFALL

Dieser and *jener* may also be used to indicate "the former" and "the latter."

Paul und Karl sind in derselben Klasse.
Paul and Karl are in the same class.

Dieser ist fleißig, jener ist faul.
The latter is diligent, the former is lazy.

Dieser refers to Karl and *jener* to Paul (further away in the sentence).

PITFALL

A few words declined like *dieser* have the ending *-en* instead of *-es* in the masculine and neuter genitive singular. This *-en* form is found infrequently in the case of *jeder* and *welcher* but often in the case of *aller, mancher,* and *solcher.*

Das war der Grund alles (*or* allen) späteren Zweifels.
That was the cause of all later doubt.

ein Beispiel solchen starken Glaubens
an example of such strong faith

EIN- WORDS

The **indefinite article** is the grammatical designation for the little word "a" ("an" before a vowel). Since it has no plural, *kein* is given to indicate plural endings.

	Masc.	Fem.	Neuter	Plural
Nom.	ein	eine	ein	keine
Gen.	eines	einer	eines	keiner
Dat.	einem	einer	einem	keinen
Acc.	einen	eine	ein	keine

Declined like *ein* are *kein* and the possessive adjectives *mein, dein, sein, ihr; unser, euer, ihr, Ihr.*

RULE

After *als* meaning "as," German omits the indefinite article.

Als Kind habe ich das oft getan.
As a child I often did that.

Sie gab mir dies als Andenken.
She gave me this as a souvenir.

Als Moslem durfte er kein Schweinefleisch essen.
As a Moslem he could eat no pork.

Als Hindu durfte er kein Rindfleisch essen.
As a Hindu he could eat no beef.

RULE

The indefinite article ("a" or "an") is not used in German before unmodified nouns denoting profession, religion, and nationality.

Unmodified	Modified
Paul ist Lehrer.	**Paul ist ein guter Lehrer.**
Paul is a teacher.	Paul is a good teacher.
Franz ist Rechtsanwalt.	**Franz ist ein teurer Rechtsan-**
Franz is a lawyer.	**walt.**
	Franz is an expensive lawyer.
Marie ist Ärztin.	**Marie ist eine bekannte Ärztin.**
Marie is a doctor.	Marie is a well-known doctor.

PITFALL

The endings on *der* words and *ein* words are the same EXCEPT in the masculine nominative and neuter nominative and accusative where *ein* words have *no* ending.

dieser Wald   **dieses Haus**
der Hund   **jedes Buch**

But:

kein Wald   **mein Haus**
ein Hund   **ihr Buch**

RULE

Use *kein* for the negative of *ein*. *Nicht ein* may only be used for emphasis in the sense of "not one."

Sie hat keinen Freund.
She has no friend (boyfriend).

Sie hat nicht einen Freund.
She doesn't have one (single) friend.

RULE

Mancher and *solcher* are *der-* words and take *der-* word endings.
They may, however, be used in the singular without ending plus *ein*
intervening between them and the noun.

---

mancher Mann *or* **manch ein Mann**
.many a man

manches Haus *or* **manch ein Haus**
many a house

In the plural only *manche Männer* and *manche Häuser* may be used.

Possessive Adjectives

PITFALL

Possessive adjectives ending in *-er* and *-r* should not be confused with *der-* word endings since the *-er* and *-r* on *ihr, unser, euer*
are part of the word itself and not an ending. Thus in the feminine
dative it is necessary to add *-er*.

Sie spricht mit ihrer Tochter.
She is speaking with her daughter.

Wir fahren mit unserer Mutter.
We are traveling with our mother.

In the three instances where *ein-* words have no endings, do
not add a *der-* word ending.

Ihr Bruder kommt morgen.
Her brother is coming tomorrow

Dein Haus ist schön.
Your house is beautiful.

PITFALL

The word *ihr* has many meanings. As a possessive adjective it can mean "her, their, *or* your." To avoid confusion remember to capitalize *Ihr* when it means "your."

Sie will jetzt ihr Lied singen.
She wants to sing her song now.

Sie wollen jetzt ihr Lied singen.
They want to sing their song now.

Sie wollen jetzt Ihr Lied singen.
You want to sing your song now.

PITFALL

Be careful not to mix the possessive adjectives for "your." Since there are three ways of saying "you" in German (See Pronouns, p. 83) there are thus three ways of saying "your." The possessive adjective that corresponds to *du* is *dein*, for *ihr* it is *euer*, and for *Sie* it is *Ihr*.

Hast du deine Bücher mitgebracht?
Have you brought your books?

Habt ihr eure Bücher mitgebracht?
Have you brought your books?

Haben Sie Ihre Bücher mitgebracht?
Have you brought your books?

In the first question you are talking to one person you know well. The second is addressed to several people with whom you are on friendly terms, and the third is a polite question to one or more persons. English no longer uses "thou" very much. If it were used it would be wrong to say, "Hast thou brought your books?" or "Have you brought thy books?" Rather, it would be necessary to say, "Hast thou brought thy books?" and "Have you brought your books?"

RULE

All possessive adjectives can modify singular or plural nouns. Since they are adjectives, they have adjective endings which depend on the case, number, and gender of the noun they modify.

(For a presentation of adjective endings, see chapter on adjectives, p. 1.)

Ich singe mein Lied.
I sing my song.

Ich singe meine Lieder.
I sing my songs.

Sie singen ihr Lied.
They're singing their song.

Sie singen ihre Lieder.
They're singing their songs.

Er hat mir seinen Traum erzählt.
He told me his dream.

Er hat mir seine Träume erzählt.
He told me his dreams.

RULE

Third person possessive adjectives (*sein, ihr*) mean "it" when referring to inanimate objects.

Der Baum hat seine Blätter verloren.
The tree has lost its leaves.

Die Blume hat ihren Duft verloren.
The flower has lost its fragrance.

Das Bild hat seine Farbe verloren.
The picture has lost its color.

PITFALL

The possessive adjective *sein* is translated as "her" when its antecedent is *Mädchen* or *Fräulein*. (See Nouns: Diminutives, p. 50)

Das Fräulein hinter der Theke sucht sein Wechselgeld.
The girl behind the counter is looking for her change.

Das Mädchen wird jetzt sein Lied singen.
The girl will now sing her song.

Note: Frequently, especially colloquially, logical gender is used instead. (See Pronouns, p. 83.)

Das Fräulein hinter der Theke sucht ihr Wechselgeld.

Das Mädchen wird jetzt ihr Lied singen.

PITFALL

German may use possessive adjectives when speaking of parts of the body and articles of clothing. It is, however, more common and idiomatic to use the definite article instead, when there is no ambiguity of reference, i.e., when it's clear who the owner is.

Er hielt den Hut in der Hand und wartete geduldig.
He held his hat in his hand and waited patiently.

Wasch und pudre dir die Füße, dann wirst du die Welt erobern.
Wash and powder your feet and you'll conquer the world. (Graffito in a Düsseldorf swimming pool)

Mach die Augen zu und denk an England.
Close your eyes and think of England. (Traditional Victorian mother's advice)

Frequently a reflexive pronoun in the dative reinforces this construction.

Ich wusch mir das Gesicht.
I washed my face.

Er hat sich den Rücken verstaucht.
He sprained his back.

PITFALL

The pronoun (usually reflexive) is in the accusative when the object is the person but it is in the dative when the part of the body is mentioned. Contrast:

Accusative	Dative
Ich wasche mich.	**Ich wasche mir die Hände.**
I wash (myself).	I wash my hands.
Ich schlage ihn.	**Ich schlage ihm auf den Kopf.**
I hit him.	I hit him in the head.

Ich rasiere mich.
I shave (myself).

Du kämmst dich nie.
You never comb (yourself).

Ich rasiere mir den Bart ab.
I shave my beard off.

Du kämmst dir nie die
Haare.
You never comb your hair.

3 ■ Conjunctions

CONJUNCTIONS

A **conjunction** is a connecting word which joins words, phrases, or clauses. The basic types are coordinating conjunctions, which do not affect word order, and subordinating conjunctions, which do.

Coordinating Conjunctions

und (and)	**aber** (but)
oder (or)	**sondern** (but) [on the contrary]
allein (but)	**denn** (for) [because]

Max und Moritz trieben Unfug und wurden bestraft.
Max and Moritz made mischief and were punished.

Kommissare ersetzten Kaiser und Könige, aber Kaffee und Kuchen gibt es noch.
Commissars replaced emperors and kings, but there is still coffee and cake.

Das ist klein aber fein.
That's small but good.

Entweder . . . oder, weder . . . noch, nicht nur . . . sondern auch are sometimes called *double* or *correlative* conjunctions.

Weder Vater noch Mutter kann kommen.
Neither father nor mother can come.

Entweder du fährst nach Wien, oder du bleibst in Berlin.
Either you go to Vienna or you stay in Berlin.

PITFALL

Bald...bald does not mean "soon" but is translated as "first ...then" or "now...now."

36

Bald lachte, bald weinte sie.
Now she laughed, now she cried.
(First she laughed, then she cried.)

RULE

Both *aber* and *sondern* mean "but." *Sondern* must be used after a negative statement when that statement is contradicted.

It is equivalent to "but instead," "but rather," "but on the contrary."

Er ist nicht klug, sondern dumm.
He's not clever but stupid.

Wir sind nicht froh, sondern traurig.
We're not glad but sad.

Sie ging nicht ins Konzert, sondern las zu Hause.
She didn't go to the concert but read at home.

"Not only . . . but also" is always expressed by *nicht nur . . . sondern auch.*

Susanne ist nicht nur schön, sondern auch intelligent und reizend.
Susanne is not only beautiful but also intelligent and charming.

PITFALL

Do not be misled into thinking that the presence of *nicht* automatically requires *sondern*. *Sondern* is never used after a positive statement.

Er ist intelligent, aber nicht ehrlich.
He is intelligent but not honest.

Further, when there is no direct contradiction, that is, when the preceding statement is not cancelled out, *aber* is used after a negative.

Sie hat es nicht getan, aber sie wollte es tun.
She didn't do it but she wanted to do it.

Sie ist nicht schön, aber reizend ist sie doch.
She's not beautiful but nevertheless she's charming.

Er ging nicht ins Konzert, aber sprach viel davon.
He didn't go to the concert but talked a lot about it.

PITFALL

The use of *allein* is chiefly literary. Do not confuse it with *allein,* meaning "alone," although "the only thing" is a cumbersome translation possibility.

Er wollte um Verzeihung bitten, allein er war zu schüchtern.
He wanted to apologize but (the only thing was) he was too shy.

Subordinating Conjunctions

A **subordinating conjunction** joins a dependent clause with a main clause.

RULE

All subordinate clauses in German are set off by commas. Every subordinate clause has the "transposed" word order, i.e., the verb is placed at the end. (See Word Order, p. 147.)

Whenever you see a subordinating conjunction it serves as a signal flag routing the verb to the end of the clause. In the case of compound verbs, the auxiliary verb is last, with the infinitive or past participle immediately preceding it. The most common subordinating conjunctions are the following:

als (when)	**ob** (whether, if)
bevor (before)	**obgleich** (although)
bis (until)	**obschon** (although)
da (since) [causal]	**obwohl** (although)
daß (that)	**seit(dem)** (since) [temporal]
ehe (before, ere)	**während** (while)
falls (in case)	**weil** (because)
nachdem (after)	**wenn** (if)

RULE

Als, wann, and *wenn* all mean "when." Each one, however, has a specific function.

Als is used for single, definite events in the past.

Sie studierte Musik, als sie in Europa war.
She studied music when she was in Europe.

Als ich in der Stadt war, ging ich oft ins Theater.
When I was in the city I often went to the theater.

Sie kauften eine Kuckucksuhr, als sie im Schwarzwald waren.
They bought a cuckoo clock when they were in the Black Forest.

Als wir in Deutschland waren, aßen wir viel Schlagsahne.
We ate a lot of whipped cream when we were in Germany.

Als Luise die Briefe ihres ungetreuen Liebhabers verbrannte
. . . (Mozart song)
When Luise burned her unfaithful lover's letters . . .

Wann is used only for questions, direct or indirect. When it introduces an indirect question it is a subordinating conjunction.

Ich weiß nicht, wann ich es machen kann.
I don't know when I can do it.

Sagen Sie ihm, wann Sie abreisen!
Tell him when you're leaving.

Wenn indicates repeated or general past, present, or future events. It is always used to express "whenever" in English.

Wenn ich in der Stadt bin, gehe ich oft ins Theater.
When(ever) I'm in the city I go to the theater often.

Wenn die Sonne schien, ging ich in den Garten.
When(ever) the sun shone I went into the garden.

Wenn der weiße Flieder wieder blüht . . .
When the white lilac blooms again . . .

Ich erkläre es ihr, wenn ich sie sehe.
I'll explain it to her when I see her.

Er wird es tun, wenn er zurückkommt.
He'll do it when he comes back.

RULE

German has two words for "if," *wenn* and *ob.* Whenever the English word "whether" can be substituted for "if," German must use *ob.*

Wenn ich jetzt kommen darf, wäre ich sehr froh.
I'd be very glad if I could come now.

Wenn er kann, wird er es machen.
If he can, he'll do it.

Er sagte, er würde ihr viel geben, wenn sie tanzen wollte.
He said he'd give her a lot if she would dance.

But:

Sagen Sie mir, ob ich jetzt kommen darf.
Tell me if (whether) I may come now.

Wissen Sie, ob er es machen kann?
Do you know if (whether) he can do it?

Herodes fragte sie, ob sie tanzen wollte.
Herod asked her if she wanted to dance.

RULE

Although *da*, *weil*, and *denn* are semantically related, remember that *da* and *weil* are subordinating conjunctions (verb at the end), whereas *denn* is a coordinating conjunction (word order not affected). A *da* or *weil* clause may begin a sentence, but it is never possible to start with *denn*, since it is the exact equivalent of the English "for" (causal).

Da (weil) er viel zu tun hatte, konnte er nicht kommen.
Since (because) he had a lot to do, he couldn't come.

Er konnte nicht kommen, denn er hatte viel zu tun.
He couldn't come for (since) he had a lot to do.

PITFALL

The conjunction *denn* can never be used as a synonym for the preposition *für*.

Tun Sie das für mich, denn ich will nicht.
Do that for me for (because) I don't want to.

PITFALL

Do not confuse *weil* (because) with *während* (during, while).

Weil ich mit ihm lange telefonierte, konnte ich die Arbeit nicht fertig machen.
Because I was on the telephone a long time with him, I couldn't finish the job.

Weil du noch da bist, solltest du es versuchen.
Because you're still there you ought to try it.

Während du mit ihm telefonierst, mache ich die Arbeit fertig.
While you're talking to him on the telephone, I'll finish the job.

Während du noch da bist, solltest du es versuchen.
While you are still there you should attempt it.

PITFALL

Word order indicates whether *da* is used as a subordinating conjunction or as an adverb.

Conjunction

Da er so plötzlich aufstand, glaubte ich er wollte gehen.
Since he stood up so suddenly, I thought he wanted to go.

Da ich die blaue Blume sah . . .
Since I saw the blue flower . . .

Adverb

Da stand er plötzlich auf.
Then he suddenly stood up.

Da sah ich die blaue Blume . . .
Then (there) I saw the blue flower . . .

PITFALL

Many English conjunctions resemble prepositions. You must therefore pay particular attention to words like "after," "since," "until," "before," and determine whether they are used as prepositions or conjunctions. In German the preposition and the conjunction often differ in form, as in *nach* and *nachdem*, *vor* and *bevor*. Remember that even when the preposition and conjunction are the same, as in *während* and *bis*, only a conjunction can introduce a clause with a subject and verb. Prepositions, on the other hand, introduce nouns or pronouns. Contrast the following examples in which prepositional phrases have been italicized.

Prepositions

Lili Marleen wartet noch *vor der Kaserne*.
Lili Marleen is still waiting in front of the barracks.

***Nach der Arbeit* ruhte er sich aus.**
After work he rested.

***Nach dem Frühstück* ging er spazieren.**
After breakfast he took a walk.

Er bleibt *bis nächste Woche*.
He'll stay until next week.

***Seit dem Tag* ist er nie wieder gekommen.**
He's never come again since that day.

***Während der Woche* arbeitet er nicht.**
He doesn't work during the week.

Conjunctions

Bevor er ankam, war sie schon fortgegangen.
Before he arrived she had already left.

Nachdem er die Arbeit beendet hatte, ging er nach Hause.
After he had finished the work he went home.

Nachdem er gefrühstückt hatte, ging er spazieren.
After eating breakfast he took a walk.

Ich warte, bis er nächste Woche kommt.
I'll wait until he comes next week.

Seitdem er gekommen ist, haben wir keine Ruhe.
We've had no rest since he's come.

Sie pflückte Rosen, während er unter dem Baum schlief.
She picked roses while he slept under the tree.

> **RULE**
>
> *Seit* can be used as both a preposition and a conjunction, although *seitdem* is the distinguishing form for the conjunction. *Seitdem* can never be used as a preposition.

Seit ich ihn gesehen, glaub' ich blind zu sein. (Chamisso)
Since seeing him, I believe I'm blind.

Seit wir sie kennen, besuchen wir sie jede Woche.
Since we've known her we visit her every week.

Since both sentences use *seit* as a conjunction, *seitdem* could be substituted.

4 ■ Nouns

NOUNS

A noun names a person, place, thing, or abstract quality.

> RULE
>
> All German nouns have a gender—masculine, feminine, or neuter. All nouns are written with a capital letter.

(For declensions, see section on Cases, Articles, *Der-* and *Ein-* Words, p. 21).

GENDER

Since there is no sure way to determine the gender of most German nouns, you should learn the gender (and plural) of each noun at the same time as the noun itself.

Many theories have been advanced as to why a noun has a particular gender but there are no simple explanations since inconsistencies and irrationalities abound. When eating in German one uses a masculine spoon (*der Löffel*), a feminine fork (*die Gabel*), and a neuter knife (*das Messer*). One word for head is masculine (*der Kopf*), while another, more literary, is neuter (*das Haupt*). It's *die Lippe* and *die Nase* (lip and nose) but *der Mund* (mouth) and *das Auge* (eye); *die Hand* but *der Finger*.

If you have studied another language and remember the gender of a noun this will not necessarily help you in German, since even the gender for basic things like sun, air, earth, water, etc., can vary from language to language. Why, for instance, should speakers of Spanish refer to that renowned borough of New York City as *el Bronx* (masculine), while speakers of German refer to *die Bronx* (feminine). Studying Latin or any of the Romance languages will not always help with the gender of the same or a closely related word even in another Romance language. "Automobile" and "origin" are feminine in French, yet masculine in Spanish. In German it's *das Auto* (neuter). "Milk" is masculine in French (*le lait*) but feminine (*la leche*) in Spanish, as it is in German (*die Milch*).

Don't be disheartened. There are some signposts (suffixes) and rules which will simplify the problem. Yet the only sure way is to learn the gender with the noun.

MULTI-GENDERED NOUNS

PITFALL

Some nouns are "double-gendered," i.e., when they have different genders, their meaning is different, too. This may seem too much of a good thing to you. Fortunately, the number of these nouns is limited. Where there are dual plural forms, they have been indicated below.

Singular	Plural
der Band (volume, book)	Bände (volumes)
das Band (bond, ribbon)	Bande (bonds, fetters)
	Bänder (ribbons)
der Erbe (heir)	Erben (heirs)
das Erbe (inheritance, heritage)	Erbschaften (inheritances)
der Flur (entrance-hall, passage)	Flure (passages)
die Flur (fields, plain)	Fluren (plains)
der Gehalt (content, capacity)	Gehalte (capacities)
das Gehalt (salary)	Gehälter (salaries)
der Heide (heathen)	
die Heide (heath)	
der Hut (hat)	Hüte (hats)
die Hut (protection)	
der Junge (boy)	
das Junge (cub, young (of animals))	
der Kiefer (jaw)	Kiefer (jaws)
die Kiefer (pine tree)	Kiefern (pines)

der Kunde (customer)
die Kunde (news, tidings)

der Laster (truck)
das Laster (vice, depravity)

der Leiter (director, leader)	Leiter (directors)
die Leiter (ladder)	Leitern (ladders)

die Mark (currency; border-
    country)
das Mark (bone marrow)

der Mensch (human being)	Menschen (human beings)
das Mensch (slut, hussy)	Menscher (sluts)

der Messer (gauge, surveyor)
das Messer (knife)

Singular	*Plural*

der Militär (military man)
das Militär (the military, armed
    services)

der Moment (moment)
das Moment (decisive factor)

der Pack (package, bundle)
das Pack (mob, rabble)

der Riese (giant)
die Riese (timber slide)

der Schild (shield)	Schilde (shields)
das Schild (signboard, business	Schilder (signs)
sign)	

der See (lake)
die See (sea, ocean)

die Steuer (tax)	Steuern (taxes)
das Steuer (rudder, helm)	Steuer (rudders)

der Stift (peg)
das Stift (old-age home)

der Tau (dew)
das Tau (rope, cable)

der Tor (fool)	Toren (fools)
das Tor (gate; goal (in games))	Tore (gates)
der Verdienst (earnings, profit)	
das Verdienst (merit, service)	
die Wehr (weapon; defense (Wehrmacht))	Wehren (arms)
das Wehr (weir; dam)	Wehre (dams)

RULE

Some nouns have a fixed gender and are used for both males and females. The pronoun must then agree grammatically.

(See Pronouns, p. 86.)

der Dienstbote (servant)	das Haupt (head (of state, the family, etc.))
der Flüchtling (refugee)	das Individuum (individual)
das Genie (genius)	das Liebchen (sweetheart)
	der Liebling (darling, favorite)
das Mitglied (member)	die Ordonnanz (orderly)
die Memme (coward)	die Wache (guard, sentry)
das Opfer (victim)	die Waise (orphan)

FRENCH-DERIVED NOUNS

For many of you who have studied or will study French or a Romance language, the following pitfalls should be avoided.

PITFALL

German has many nouns derived from French. French feminines are feminine in German also but many French masculines are neuter.

das Bonbon	das Portefeuille
das Café	das Portemonnaie

With the exception of *der Zement*, French masculines in *-et* and *-ment* are neuter in German:

das Ballett, das Abonnement, das Engagement

PITFALL

French masculine nouns in *-age* are feminine in German:

die Etage (floor, story), **die Gage** (salary), **die Garage.**

PITFALL

In the Romance languages the last noun in a compound noun does not determine gender, as is the case in German. (See Compound Nouns, p. 52.)

In French it's *la pluie* but *le parapluie, la feuille* and *la monnaie* but *le portefeuille* and *le portemonnaie.* In Spanish it's *la voz* but *el portavoz.* German **das Geld** + **die Tasche** will yield **die Geldtasche.**

SUFFIXES AND OTHER GENDER INDICATORS

Although it must be repeated that the best and only sure way to master gender is to learn it with the noun, the following should be helpful.

MASCULINE NOUNS

1. the seven days of the week (*Montag, Dienstag,* etc.) and all nouns ending in *-tag,* such as *Arbeitstag, Feiertag* (See Compound Nouns.)

2. the twelve months of the year (*Januar, Februar,* etc.)

3. points of the compass (*der Norden, der Süden,* etc.)

4. nouns formed from verbal stems without an added suffix, for example, *Anfang, Fall, Befehl, Rat*

5. nouns of more than one syllable ending in *-ig, -ich,* and *-ing,* for example, *Teppich, Honig, Hering, Feigling*

6. nouns of occupation ending in *-er, -or, -ler* or *-ner,* for example, *Brauer, Bäcker, Pastor, Bettler, Schaffner*

FEMININE NOUNS

1. most two-syllable nouns ending in *-e,* for example, *Sonne, Lampe, Straße, Katze, Blume*

Exceptions: Junge, Neffe (obviously, since they refer to masculine beings), *der Friede, der Funke, der Glaube, der Name, der Same;* also *das Auge,* and *das Ende*

2. nouns of more than one syllable ending in *-ei, -heit* (or *keit*), *-in, -kunft, -ion, -schaft, -tät, -ung,* for example, *Heuchelei, Dummheit, Ehrlichkeit, Auskunft, Verwandtschaft, Elektrizität, Nation, Landung*

NEUTER NOUNS

1. all nouns identical with infinitives (verbal nouns), for example, *das Essen, das Trinken, das Tanzen.* Note that verbal nouns do not have plural forms.

2. most countries, towns, and cities.

Exceptions: die Schweiz, die Tschechoslowakei, die Türkei and the following masculines: *Irak, Iran, Jemen, Kongo, Libanon, Sudan.* The definite article *die* is always used with the three feminines and usually with the masculines.

Although Deutschland and Rußland are neuter (das Land), the nouns *Republik* and *Union* are feminine. Thus: *die Bundesrepublik Deutschland (die BRD), die Deutsche Demokratische Republik (die DDR)* and *die Sowjetunion (die UdSSR). Die USA* and *Die Vereinigten Staaten* are plural.

3. most terms for the young, for example, *das Baby, das Kind, das Kalb, das Ferkel, das Füllen*

4. nouns ending in *-tum*

Exceptions: der Reichtum and *der Irrtum*

5. all nouns ending in *-chen* or *lein*

6. all fractions with the exception of *die Hälfte,* for example, *das Drittel, das Neuntel*

7. letters of the alphabet, for example, *ein großes F, das hohe C*

8. most nouns with the prefix *Ge-* but there are many exceptions, for example, *der Gesang, Geschmack, Geruch* and *die Gemeinde, Geschichte, Gestalt, Gewalt*

FEMININE SUFFIXES

It is particularly important that you fix the feminine suffixes in your mind since they take care of some of the problem of genders for you. Many nouns can be formed by adding these suffixes and the gender is predictable. Many of them are like the English suffixes *-hood, -ness, -ty, -ship.*

> RULE
>
> English *-er* may be both masculine and feminine. In German it is only masculine.

If a doctor, lawyer, teacher, etc., is a woman, remember to "feminize" the noun by adding *-in* and adding an umlaut if possible.

der Lehrer (male teacher)
die Lehrerin (female teacher)

der Arzt (male doctor)
die Ärztin (female doctor)

der Rechtsanwalt (male lawyer)
die Rechtsanwältin (female lawyer)

For a female professor both *sie ist Professorin* and *sie ist Professor* can be used. When a woman is a medical doctor she is called an *Ärztin* or a *Doktorin.* But for a female Ph.D., *sie ist Doktor der Philosophie* is used

DIMINUTIVES

English diminutives ending in *-y, -et* or *-ette, -ling,* and *-kin* (dolly, rivulet, floret, princeling, etc.) exist, but are less frequently used than German *-chen* and *-lein.*

> RULE
>
> All nouns ending in *-chen* or *-lein* are neuter, irrespective of logical gender.

das Mädchen (girl)   **Mütterchen** (mommy, old lady)
das Fräulein (girl, miss)   **Väterchen** (daddy)

Mütterchen and *Väterchen* have the connotation of endearment (one function of the diminutives) and sometimes of advanced years. When diminutives are added remember to umlaut the noun if possible. *Was Hänschen nicht lernt, lernt Hans nimmermehr* may be translated freely as "*If Johnny doesn't learn it John never will.*"

When called upon to write a composition in German it may be tempting to "neutralize" the troublesome problem of gender by adding *-chen* or *-lein* to nouns but this should not be done indiscriminately since the result would be affected and cutesy.

In Northern Germany *-chen* is preferred. Dialect variations of *-lein* prevail in the South, *-erl* and *-el* in Austria, *-le* in Swabia, and *-li* in Switzerland. Because of the fairy tale, the forms Hänsel and Gretel are probably more familiar to you than Hänschen and Gretchen.

VERBAL NOUNS

> RULE
>
> It is necessary to distinguish between English *-ing* as a verbal noun (gerund) or as an adjective or adverb (present participle.)
> German verbal nouns are identical with the infinitive. They are all neuter, and like all nouns in German, are capitalized. Verbal nouns do not have plurals. The present participle adds a *-d* to the infinitive and is used adjectivally or adverbially, i.e., with appropriate endings.

-ing used as a verbal noun:

Sie sollten das Rauchen und das Trinken lassen.
You should give up smoking and drinking.

Das hat mit ihrem Singen die Lorelei getan. (Heine)
Lorelei did that with her singing.

Fliegen ist nichts für mich.
Flying is nothing for me.

-ing used adjectivally or adverbially (present participle):

Die ganze Nacht stand er rauchend und trinkend an der Bar.
He stood at the bar drinking and smoking all night.

Die singenden Hunde treten jetzt auf.
The singing dogs will now perform.

,,Der Fliegende Holländer" ist eine Oper von Wagner.
The Flying Dutchman is an opera by Wagner.

Bach's Cantata #12 *Weinen, Klagen* speaks of "weeping, lamenting." These are verbal nouns. If you wish to use them as adjectives or adverbs you have to use the present participle, for example, *Weinend und klagend verließ sie ihren Geliebten,* or *Weeping and lamenting she left her lover.*

> ## PITFALL
>
> Verbal nouns may be easier for you to handle, because they are all neuter, but remember they emphasize the action itself and are usually translated by *-ing*. Be sure to learn the regular nouns.
>
> | | |
> |---|---|
> | **das Bad** (bath) | **das Baden** (bathing) |
> | **der Tanz** (dance) | **das Tanzen** (dancing) |
> | **das Lied** (song) | **das Singen** (singing) |
> | **das Getränk** (drink) | **das Trinken** (drinking) |

COMPOUND NOUNS

The very sight of some German compound nouns may frighten you. They may appear monstrous and cumbersome, may compound your confusion and make you want to pound your head against the dictionary. But if you can recognize the components you will find that they are often quite simple. Compound nouns can be used for ordinary, everyday things. A Lufthansa German Airlines ad for the "Air Travel Card", for example, contains the following:

keine Grund- oder Bearbeitungsgebühr
no basic charge or handling fee

rationelle Reisekostenabrechnung
simplified, cost-saving travel accounting

keine Wertbegrenzung
no limit to amount spent

gültig für Flugscheine und Übergepäck
good for flight tickets and excess baggage

gültig als Kreditreferenz für Hotelketten und Mietwagenunternehmen
good as a credit reference for hotel chains and car rental companies

Most of these compounds are not difficult to recognize with a little dictionary work. *Kreditreferenz* and *Hotelketten* are simple compounds. You might not, for instance, find *Übergepäck* but it is not difficult to figure out since *Gepäck* is *baggage*.

Perhaps the tendency of German to form compound nouns is partly responsible for the large number of philosophical poems in German. The twentieth-century poet Christian Morgenstern is best known for his widely popular humorous and satiric verse. His many philosophical poems, which were of more concern and interest to him, are not well known at all. One brief example will suffice:

> **Aus Riesenschöpfungsüberblicken**
> **aus Aufschau zu verborgnen Bildnersphären**
> **aus Selbstmiteinbezug in deren Stufen —**
> **ein Mitgefühl mit dieser Welt Geschicken.**

Such "poetry" is best translated by a prose paraphrase: "From the transcendental contemplation of immense creative forces, from a looking up to hidden realms of creativity, from self-inclusion and involvement in the stages of those creative processes there arises an empathic identification with the events and destinies of this world." The same Morgenstern could write a little poem on the tenses drinking champagne and toasting the future:

> ***Unter Zeiten***
>
> **Das Perfekt und das Imperfekt**
> **tranken Sekt**
> **Sie stießen aufs Futurum an**
> **(was man wohl gelten lassen kann).**
> **Plusquamper und Exaktfutur**
> **blintzen nur.**

RULE

The last noun in a compound noun always determines the gender for the whole noun, no matter what gender the other noun or nouns may be.

Thus, *die Geburt* (birth), *der Tag* (day), and *das Geschenk* (present) can combine to *der Geburtstag* (birthday) or *das Geburtstagsgeschenk* (birthday present).

die Schule + *das* Mädchen = *das* Schulmädchen (schoolgirl)

das Mädchen + *die* Schule = *die* Mädchenschule (girls' school)

die Kunst + *das* Werk = *das* Kunstwerk (work of art)

der Zahn + *die* Bürste = *die* Zahnbürste (toothbrush)

der Zahn + *das* Fleisch = *das* Zahnfleisch (gums)

der Zahn + *der* Arzt = *der* Zahnarzt (dentist (male))

der Zahn + *die* Ärztin = *die* Zahnärztin (dentist (female))

RULE

Often an *n* or *s* is used to link compound nouns. Although the ending *s* is associated with the genitive singular of masculine and neuter nouns (see declensions of articles in the chapter on Cases, articles, p. 24), this *Bindungs-* or "connective" *s* can join nouns of any gender, including feminines, in forming compound nouns.

---

die Wahrheitsliebe (love of truth)

die Ansichtskarte (scenic postcard)

die Kündigungsfrist (notice of termination of employment)

die Liebeserklärung (declaration of love)

PITFALL

The rule that the last noun in a compound noun determines its gender is valid, but there are inconsistencies. *Mut, Teil, Meter* and *Woche* should be noted.

About half the compounds of *der Mut* are feminine.

Masculine	Feminine
der Edelmut	*die* Anmut
Freimut	Demut
Gleichmut	Großmut
Hochmut	Langmut
Kleinmut	Sanftmut
Übermut	Schwermut
Wankelmut	Wehmut

Mut means *courage; state of mind.* Although states of mind can vary and change rapidly, often irrationally, it is difficult to account for the irrationality of the fact that *Großmut,* meaning *magnanimity, generosity* is feminine, whereas *Kleinmut,* meaning *pusillanimity, narrow-mindedness; despondency* is masculine.

PITFALL

Der Teil is usually masculine in modern German except in fixed phrases like *ich für mein Teil* where it is neuter. Some compounds are neuter, however.

das Abteil	Hinterteil
Erbteil	Vorderteil
Gegenteil	

Note: Vorteil (advantage) and *Nachteil* (disadvantage) are masculine.

PITFALL

Meter, Millimeter and *Zentimeter* are officially neuter. Despite this, they are usually masculine in colloquial speech. In Switzerland they are officially masculine. The compounds *Kilometer* and *Gasometer* are masculine, whereas *Barometer* and *Thermometer* are neuter. *Liter,* too, is officially neuter but colloquially masculine.

RULE

All the days of the week are masculine, including *Mittwoch,* even though *die Woche* is feminine.

Wednesday, as its English name indicates, was sacred to Wotan or Woden, chief of the Germanic gods. *Mittwoch* (midweek) is a neutral, monkish substitution in German. Christianity attempted to eliminate so-called pagan elements from the language. *Freitag* "Friday," for instance, was sacred to Freia, a Germanic goddess associated with love and beauty. Christianity tried to associate Friday instead with the Virgin Mary and to make it a day of fasting and abstinence.

NOUN PLURALS

Just as you should always learn a new noun with its gender you should, similarly, learn the plural at the same time. There are a few English nouns which do not form plurals in -*s*. Among these plurals are: *oxen, geese, mice, men, children, lice.*

> **RULE**
>
> German nouns either remain unchanged or may add -*e*, -*er*, -*en*, or in a very few instances -*s*. Many take an umlaut, and thus change their sound.

NOUN PLURALS IN -S

> **RULE**
>
> German noun plurals in -*s* are mainly of non-Germanic origin. **They never take an umlaut or add an -*n* to the dative plural.**

You should have no trouble recognizing them.

Autos	Schecks
Kameras	Parks
Hotels	Babys

Some nouns also have a colloquial plural in -*s*, especially in Northern Germany, in addition to their official plural. Among these are the masculines *Bengel, Junge, Kerl, Onkel,* and the neuters *Fräulein* and *Mädel.* A few marine words also add -*s* in the plural: *der Kai, das Deck,* and *das Dock.*

> **RULE**
>
> German nouns add -*n* to the dative plural unless they already have one. Noun plurals in -*s* do not.

mit den Details	in den Restaurants
aus den Autos	von den besten Hotels

PITFALL

When you see an -*s* on a German noun it is much more likely to be the genitive singular of a masculine or neuter noun than a plural. (For cases and noun declensions see the chapter, "Cases, Articles, Der- and Ein- Words," p. 21)

die Spielsachen des Kindes	**die Seiten des Buches**
the child's toys	the pages of the book
die Zweige des Baumes	**die Fenster des Hauses**
the branches of the tree	the windows of the house

RULE

To show possession -*s* is also added to proper nouns. Although this -*s* is a masculine and neuter genitive ending, it is also added to feminine nouns. Unlike English, no apostrophe is used.

Vaters Pfeife	**Mutters Kochrezepte**
father's pipe	mother's recipes
Lulus Apfelstrudel	**Deutschlands Wälder**
Lulu's apple strudel	Germany's forests

Note: If a name ends in -*s*, -*ß*, -*x*, -*z*, or -*tz* an apostrophe *is* used, but no extra *s* is added, as in English.

Brahms' Lieder	**Max und Moritz' Streiche**
Brahms's songs	Max and Moritz's pranks
Flex' Roman	**Curtius' Geschichte**
Flex's novel	Curtius's history

Types of Noun Plurals

GROUP I

RULE

Group I nouns have no ending in the plural. Masculines often take an umlaut, neuters never do. The two feminines in this group take an umlaut.

This group consists of the following:

1. Masculines and neuters in -*el*. -*en*. or -*er*

Singular	Plural	Singular	Plural
der Beutel	die Beutel	das Kabel	die Kabel
Garten	Gärten	Kissen	Kissen
Lehrer	Lehrer	Zimmer	Zimmer

    Exceptions are **der Vetter -die Vettern** and **der Bauer -die Bauern.**

2. Neuter nouns ending in the diminutive suffixes -*chen* and -*lein* (See Diminutives in this section.)

3. Only two feminines, *Mutter* pl. *Mütter* and *Tochter.* pl. *Töchter*

> ## PITFALL
>
> Many **GROUP I** nouns have identical forms in the nominative singular and the genitive plural. *Der Maler* may thus mean "the painter" or "of the painters." You must pay attention to the context, especially when inverted word order is used.
>
> **Die Aufgaben der Schüler korrigierte der Lehrer.**
> The teacher corrected the students' assignments.

> ## PITFALL
>
> Since plural forms of nouns in Group I are either exactly the same as or only slightly different (umlaut) from the singular, you must pay careful attention to the verb and the preceding article or word which indicates case in order to determine whether it is singular or plural. Contrast:
>
> *Singular*
>
> **Der Sänger beginnt.**
> The singer begins.
>
> **Kein Kabel ist gekommen.**
> No cable has come.
>
> **Das Zimmer wurde gereinigt.**
> The room was cleaned.
>
> **Welches Mädchen haben Sie gesehen?**
> Which girl did you see?

Plural

Die Sänger beginnen.
The singers begin.

Keine Kabel sind gekommen.
No cables have come.

Die Zimmer wurden gereinigt.
The rooms were cleaned.

Welche Mädchen haben Sie gesehen?
Which girls did you see?

GROUP II

RULE

Noun plurals in **Group II** end in -e.

This group consists of the following:

1. Most one-syllable masculines

Singular	Plural	Singular	Plural
Baum	Bäume	Sohn	Söhne
Brief	Briefe	Stuhl	Stühle
Freund	Freunde	Tag	Tage
Schuh	Schuhe	Tisch	Tische

2. Many one-syllable feminines

Frucht	Früchte	Nacht	Nächte
Hand	Hände	Stadt	Städte
Kraft	Kräfte	Wand	Wände

3. A few monosyllabic neuters

Jahr	Jahre	Schwein	Schweine
Meer	Meere	Stück	Stücke
Pferd	Pferde	Tier	Tiere

4. A few polysyllabic masculines and neuters

der Abend	Abende	*das* Geschenk	Geschenke
Bleistift	Bleistifte	Gefühl	Gefühle
König	Könige	Gesetz	Gesetze
Monat	Monate	Gedicht	Gedichte

The masculines sometimes take an umlaut, the neuters never do. The feminines take an umlaut if possible (*ä. ö. ü. äu*).

Dative -*e*

> RULE
>
> As a rule, feminine nouns never add anything to their singular forms. One-syllable masculine and neuter nouns may, however, add an -*e* to the dative singular.

This -*e* is optional and its use is declining even in Northern Germany where it is more common. It is most frequently found in phrases like *nach Hause, zu Hause, auf dem Lande,* although here, too, the -*e* is optional.

PITFALL

Do not confuse an optional -*e* on a dative singular with plural forms.

Singular

Dem Hunde hat er nie etwas Gutes zu fressen gegeben.
He never gave the dog anything good to eat.

Auf dem Tische liegen Bücher.
Books are lying on the table.

Plural

Die Hunde haben nie etwas Gutes zu fressen bekommen.
The dogs never got anything good to eat.

Die Tische sind neu.
The tables are new.

> RULE
>
> The neuters in **GROUPS I** and **II** never take an umlaut.

Many masculines take an umlaut, but many do not. Contrast the following masculine noun plurals.

GROUP I

Umlaut	No Umlaut
Äpfel (apples)	**Adler** (eagles)
Äcker (fields)	**Dampfer** (steamships)
Gärten (gardens)	**Schatten** (shadows)

GROUP II

Gründe (reasons)	**Hunde** (dogs)
Verträge (treaties)	**Tage** (days)
Gäste (guests)	**Abende** (evenings)
Söhne (sons)	**Monate** (months)
Bäume (trees)	**Onkel** (uncles)
Stühle (chairs)	**Schuhe** (shoes)

GROUP III

> **RULE**
>
> Nouns in **Group III** end in *-er* in the plural. They always take an umlaut (where possible).

1. Most monosyllabic neuters and all nouns in *-tum*

das Bild	Bilder	Haus	Häuser
Buch	Bücher	Licht	Lichter
Dorf	Dörfer	Volk	Völker
Feld	Felder	*der* Irrtum	Irrtümer

2. A few one-syllable masculines

Geist	Geister	Rand	Ränder
Gott	Götter	Wald	Wälder
Leib	Leiber	Wurm	Würmer
Mann	Männer		

GROUP IV

> **RULE**
>
> **Group IV** nouns end in *-en*. They never take an umlaut in the plural but may, of course, already have one in the singular and retain it in the plural. Nouns ending in *-e, -el, -er* in the singular add *-n*. Others add *-en*.

In this group are the following:

1. Most masculine and feminine nouns of more than one syllable

Singular	Plural	Singular	Plural
der Knabe	Knaben	Philosoph	Philosophen
Junge	Jungen	Professor	Professoren
Jude	Juden	Intendant	Intendanten
Franzose	Franzosen	Reisende	Reisenden
Löwe	Löwen	Kranke	Kranken
Pianist	Pianisten	Gefangene	Gefangenen
die Universität	Universitäten	Schwester	Schwestern
Klasse	Klassen	Minute	Minuten
Blume	Blumen	Zeitung	Zeitungen
Feder	Federn	Königin	Königinnen

2. Some monosyllabic masculines and feminines

der Held	Helden	Fürst	Fürsten
Herr	Herren	Graf	Grafen
Mensch	Menschen	Ochs	Ochsen
Narr	Narren	Schmerz	Schmerzen
die Frau	Frauen	Uhr	Uhren
Tür	Türen	Zeit	Zeiten

3. GROUP IV neuter nouns are few in number

Auge	Augen	Bett	Betten
Ohr	Ohren	Hemd	Hemden
Herz	Herzen		

> **PITFALL**
>
> **Group IV** masculines end in *-n* or *-en* in all cases, singular and plural, except the nominative. *Herr* has *Herrn* in the singular and *Herren* in the plural. A few like *das Herz* and *der Schmerz* have *-ens* in the genitive singular. Remember that feminine nouns in *-in* double the *n* before adding the plural *-en*.

Königin (queen)	Lehrerin (teacher)
Königinnen (queens)	Lehrerinnen (teachers)
Freundin (friend)	Gräfin (countess)
Freundinnen (friends)	Gräfinnen (countesses)

> **PITFALL**
>
> Singular and plural forms of masculine nouns in Group IV can easily be confused since they both end in *-n* or *-en*. Again it is necessary to pay attention to syntax.
>
> **Sie hat den Studenten geheiratet.**
> She married the student.
>
> **Sie hat mit den Studenten getanzt.**
> She danced with the students.

Special Cases

> **PITFALL**
>
> Some nouns have two plurals with different meanings.

Singular	Plural
das Band (bond; ribbon)	Bande (bonds)
	Bänder (ribbons)
die Bank (bench; bank (finance))	Bänke (benches)
	Banken (banks)
der Bau (building; burrow)	Bauten (buildings)
	Baue (burrows)
das Ding (thing; female creature (humorously or pejoratively))	Dinge (things)
	Dinger (female creatures)

der Druck (print; pressure)	Drucke (things printed (as in Neudrucke reprints)) Drücke (pressures)
das Gesicht (apparition; face)	Gesichte (apparitions) Gesichter (faces)
das Land (land, country)	Lande (lands, regions (literary)) Länder (lands, countries)
der Mann (man; vassal)	Männer (men) Mannen (vassals (poetic or humorous))
die Mutter (mother; bolt, screw)	Mütter (mothers) Muttern (bolts)
der Rat (council; councillor; counsel, advice)	Räte (councils; councillors) Ratschläge (counsels)
der Strauß (ostrich; bouquet)	Strauße (ostriches) Sträuße (bouquets)
das Wort (word)	Worte (words (connected, related)) Wörter (words (unrelated))
der Zoll (customs duty; inch)	Zölle (customs duties) vier Zoll (four inches)

PITFALL

A few German nouns have special plurals or no real plural of their own. Sometimes *-artikel* or *-sachen* are added. Thus *Raubfälle, Todesfälle, Unglücksfälle* refer to "instances" of robbery, death, and accident. *Schmucksachen* and *Spielsachen* are "things" used to adorn or to play with.

Singular	Plural
der Atem (breath)	Atemzüge
das Bestreben (effort)	Bestrebungen
der Betrug (deception)	Betrügereien
die Furcht (fear)	Befürchtungen

der Glaube (belief, faith)	Glaubensartikel, Glaubenssätze
der Kohl (cabbage)	Kohlköpfe
das Lob (praise)	Lobsprüche
der Luxus (luxury)	Luxusartikel
der Raub (theft)	Raubfälle
der Schmuck (jewelry)	Schmucksachen, Schmuckstücke
das Spielzeug (toy)	Spielsachen
der Tod (death)	Todesfälle
das Unglück (accident)	Unglücksfälle
das Unternehmen (enterprise)	Unternehmungen
das Versprechen (promise)	Versprechungen
der Zank (quarrel)	Zänkereien

RULE

Nouns like *Eltern, Ferien, Geschwister, Kosten, Leute,* and *Möbel* are used only in the plural.

Seine Eltern leben noch.
His parents are still alive.

Ich freue mich auf die Sommerferien.
I'm looking forward to summer vacation.

Er hat viele Geschwister.
He has many brothers and sisters.

Was werden die Leute sagen?
What will people say?

PITFALL

Some nouns are singular in German and plural in English. Thus you must be careful to use a singular verb form in German.

Die Polizei hat den Mörder gefangen.
The police have captured the murderer.

Das Volk will Brot.
The people want bread.

Das ist eine neue Brille.
Those are new glasses.

The more common of these nouns are listed here:

die Asche (ashes)
der Bodensatz (dregs, lees)
die Brille (eyeglasses)
der Dank (thanks)
die Dynamik (dynamics)
die Familie (family)
das Feuerwerk (fireworks)
der Hafer (oats)
die Hose (pair of pants)
der Inhalt (contents)
die Kaserne (barracks)
die Mathematik (mathematics)
das Mittelalter (the Middle Ages)
die Nachricht (news)

die Physik (physics)
die Polizei (police)
das Quartier (quarters)
die Schere (pair of scissors)
die Statistik (statistics)
die Treppe (stairs)
die Umgebung (surroundings, neighborhood)
die Umgegend (surroundings)
das Unkraut (weed, weeds)
das Volk (people)
das Werk (works, factory)
die Zange (pair of tongs)

PITFALL

Weihnachten (Christmas), *Ostern* (Easter), and *Pfingsten* (Pentecost) may be plural or singular. They are most frequently plural but when used as the subject of a sentence they are followed by a singular verb.

Thus *Fröhliche Weihnachten!* is more common than the singular *Fröhliches Weihnachten!*

But: Weihnachten fällt immer auf den 25. Dezember.
Christmas falls on the 25th of December.

Ostern wird im Frühling gefeiert.
Easter is celebrated in the spring.

5 ■ Prepositions

PREPOSITIONS

A preposition is a word used with a noun, pronoun, infinitive, or adverb to indicate a relationship to another word in a sentence or phrase. Prepositions frequently express a spatial relationship between people or things.

> **Ich habe ihn lieber als Feind vor mir denn als Freund hinter mir.**
> I'd rather have him as an enemy before me than as a friend behind me.
> (Heine on the poet Platen)

> **Über den Fluß und in die Bäume**
> Across the river and into the trees

German has prepositions which take or "govern" the genitive, dative, or accusative. There is, in addition, a fourth group, the most difficult, which can take either the dative or the accusative. With the exception of this last group (called in many texts either "doubtful" or "two-way" prepositions), the use of a particular case is fixed. It *is* necessary, however, to memorize prepositions. Some teachers use the traditional litanies accompanied by mnemonic devices like "*aus, außer, bei, mit, nach, seit, von, zu* take the dative; they sure do" and "*bis, durch, für, gegen ohne, um, wider* take the accusative, and don't you forget it either."

Prepositions are best learned, however, with their objects, i.e., in prepositional phrases. There are many famous examples of prepositional phrases in a musical context. Baron Ochs, in the second act of Richard Strauss' *Der Rosenkavalier,* waltzes about vaunting his romantic prowess. He repeats *mit mir* and *ohne mich* frequently. The girl he's currently pursuing will be ecstatic with him and unsatisfied without him (*mit mir keine Nacht dir zu lang*), he asserts. Other examples are *Durch die Wälder durch die Auen (Der Freischütz),* or . . . *was hast du für mich getan (Fidelio).*

Prepositions with the Genitive

während (during)
wegen (because of, on account of)
statt (anstatt) (instead of)
trotz (in spite of)
diesseits (on this side of)
jenseits (on the other side of, beyond)
beiderseits (on both sides of)
. . . halber (for the sake of, because of)
innerhalb (inside, within)
außerhalb (outside of)
oberhalb (above)
unterhalb (below)
um . . . willen (for the sake of)

Other prepositions take the genitive but are used mainly in official or commercial language. Colloquially many are used with the dative although "of" is often part of their translation. The phrases *trotz allem* (despite everything) and *trotz alledem* (despite all that) are fixed with the dative. *Trotz des schlechten Wetters* (Despite the bad weather) is, however, preferable to *Trotz dem schlechten Wetter*. This is true of all the prepositions with the genitive. There is, however, a tendency to substitute the dative because the genitive is often thought to sound stilted. (See Verbs with a Genitive Object in the chapter on Verbs, p. 137.)

The two-part preposition *um . . . willen* has the noun in the middle.

um Gottes willen
for God's sake

um des Reimes willen
for the sake of the rhyme

> PITFALL
>
> *Während* may be either a preposition (during) or a conjunction (while, whereas). (See Conjunctions, p. 36.)
>
> Preposition
> **Während des Tages bleibt er zu Hause.**
> During the day he stays home.

Während der Nacht arbeitet sie.
During the night she works.

Conjunction
Vater trinkt gern Schnaps, während Mutter lieber Wein trinkt.
Father likes to drink hard liquor while mother prefers wine.

Während du das Essen vorbereitest, mach ich einen Spaziergang.
While you prepare the meal, I'll take a walk.

Prepositions with the Dative

The most common prepositions with the dative are the following:

aus (out of, from)
außer (outside; except, besides)
bei (near, by, with)
mit (with)
nach (after, according to)
seit (since)
von (from, of, by)
zu (to, at)

RULE

The preposition *seit* is used for "since" only in reference to time. In a causal sense the subordinating conjunction *da* is used.

Ich habe ihn seit gestern nicht gesehen.
I haven't seen him since yesterday.

Da ich ihn seit gestern nicht gesehen habe, . . .
Since I haven't seen him since yesterday, . . .

(For further confusions between prepositions and conjunctions, see Conjunctions, p. 41.)

PITFALL

When going "to" a town or a country, the most frequent preposition used is *nach*. It is used before all neuter countries. In the case of the three feminine countries, *in* + accusative is used.

Wir fahren nach Deutschland (Italien, Spanien, Rußland, England).
We travel to Germany (Italy, Spain, Russia, England).

But:

Wir fahren in die Schweiz (in die Türkei, in die Tschechoslowakei).
We go to Switzerland (Turkey, Czechoslovakia).

Do not use *zu* with countries.

RULE

Use *von* or *durch* not *bei* to express the agent in the passive.

Das Lied wurde von ihr gesungen.
The song was sung by her.

Er wurde durch dieses Medikament geheilt.
He was cured by this medication.

PITFALL

Bei is often used in the same sense as French *chez* which, in turn, enjoys some popularity in English. But unlike *chez*, it is never used with verbs of motion.

Ich wohne bei meinem Onkel.
I live at my uncle's house.

But:

Ich gehe zu meinem Onkel.
I'm going to my uncle.

Er hat über das Griechische bei Goethe und das Dämonische bei Hoffmann geschrieben.
He wrote on the Greek element in Goethe's and the demonic in Hoffman's works.

Bei, like most German prepositions, has a variety of idiomatic translations.

> **RULE**
>
> Use *mit* not *bei* to express the means by which one travels.

Wir fahren mit dem Schiff.   We're traveling by ship.
mit dem Zug   by train
mit dem Wagen   by car

"By Air Mail" is *Mit Luftpost*. In Austria and Switzerland *Mit Flugpost* is often used. For travel by air, only *fliegen* is used.

Prepositions with the Accusative

The most common prepositions with the accusative are the following:

bis (till, until, as far as)
durch (through)
für (for)
gegen (against)
ohne (without)
um (around, round about)

> **RULE**
>
> *Bis* is frequently followed by another preposition which determines the case. If *zu* follows, the noun is in the dative.

Wir gingen bis zur Tür.
We went as far as the door.

PITFALL

Do not confuse the prepositions *für* and *vor. Vor* means "in front of, before," and translates as "for" only in a few idioms. In time expressions, *vor* + dative means "ago."

Sie tanzte vor Freude.
She danced for joy.

Nimm dich in acht vor blonden Schauspielerinnen!
Watch out for blonde actresses!

Er ist vor einer Stunde angekommen.
He arrived an hour ago.

PITFALL

"For all," meaning "despite," is never expressed by *für alle* in German. Use *trotz* + genitive.

Rosen, trotz ihrer Dornen, sind schön.
For all their thorns, roses are beautiful.

Trotz aller Schmerzen ist das Leben herrlich.
For all its sorrows, life is splendid.

PITFALL

Although the preposition *für* always takes the accusative, in the construction *was für ein-* (what kind of), case is determined by use in the sentence.

Was für ein Wunsch ist das?   (*Wunsch* is in the nominative.)
What kind of a wish is that?

Was für eine Blume wollen   (*Blume* is the direct object and
Sie?   thus accusative)
What sort of a flower do you want?

Was für einem Mann haben   (*Mann* is the indirect object and
Sie das Geld gegeben?   thus in the dative.)
To what sort of a man did you give the money?

PITFALL

Gegen and *wider* take the accusative; *entgegen* and *zuwider* take the dative. All mean "against." *Gegen* is more commonly used than the others.

Gegen alle Erwartungen setzte er sich durch.
Allen Erwartungen entgegen setzte er sich durch.
Against (contrary to) all expectations, he prevailed.

wider meine Befehle
meinen Befehlen zuwider
against my orders

Entgegen usually follows and *zuwider* always does.

PITFALL

The position of a preposition is, by definition, before the word to which it refers. Some prepositions, however, can come after that word. They are then called *postpositions*. When *nach* is used as a postposition, it means "according to."

Seiner Meinung nach ist es schon zu spät.
In his opinion it's already too late.

Other less common prepositions with the dative are generally used as postpositions. They are the following:

gemäß (in accordance with)   **zufolge** (as the result of)
gegenüber (opposite)   **zuliebe** (for the sake of)
Tun Sie das mir zuliebe!
Do that for my sake (to please me).

Entlang and *hindurch* both take the accusative.

Er wanderte den Bach entlang.
He wandered (strolled) along the brook.

The preposition *wegen* (+ genitive) may be placed before or after the word to which it refers. *Halber,* also with the genitive, always follows the word to which it refers.

wegen der guten Küche
der guten Küche wegen
der guten Küche halber
All mean "because of the good cuisine."

Prepositions with Either Dative or Accusative

RULE

Some prepositions may take either the dative or the accusative.

They are the following:

an (to, at, in, by)   **in** (in, into)
auf (on, upon, to)   **neben** (next to, beside)
hinter (behind)   **über** (over, across)

unter (under, below)
vor (before, in front of)
zwischen (between)

These prepositions take the accusative when the verb indicates motion toward a goal or destination and the dative when it does not. If the verb answers the question *wo?* (where?) the preposition takes the dative. If it answers the question *wohin?* (whereto?, whither?) the preposition takes the accusative.

ACCUSATIVE

Er setzt sich auf den Stuhl.
He sits down on the chair.

Sie legt das Buch auf den Tisch.
She lays (places) the book onto the table.

DATIVE

Er sitzt auf dem Stuhl.
He is sitting on the chair.

Das Buch liegt auf dem Tisch.
The book is lying on the table.

With verbs like *sitzen* and *liegen* one can expect the dative, since they denote static conditions—they indicate "place where." *Setzen* and *legen* are causative verbs, i.e., if one sets or lays something somewhere one causes it to sit or to lie. In the first accusative example above, he is not on the chair, but on the way to it. In the second, the book is not yet on the table but on its way there. After verbs like *stehen, bleiben, sein, liegen,* and *sitzen,* one can expect a dative with the doubtful prepositions, and after verbs like *gehen, springen, setzen, legen, stecken,* and *kommen,* an accusative.

Accusative

Ich gehe heute ins Kino, morgen in die Oper.
I'm going to the movies today, tomorrow to the opera.

Wir gehen an die See.
We're going to the sea.

Der Hausknecht warf ihn vor die Tür.
The bouncer threw him out. (literally in front of the door)

Lili Marleen geht unter die Laterne.
Lili Marleen is going (to a place) underneath the streetlight.

Dative

Ich war heute im Kino; morgen bin ich in der Oper.
I was in the movies today; tomorrow I'll be in (at) the opera.

Wir verbringen unsere Ferien an der See.
We spend our vacation at the seashore.

Er liegt jetzt vor der Tür.
He's lying in front of the door now.

Lili Marleen steht unter der Laterne.
Lili Marleen is standing underneath the streetlight.

PITFALL

Although it is correct to associate verbs which indicate motion to a place with the accusative case for the doubtful prepositions, it is possible for motion to be confined within a place, and thus to use the dative.

Der Lehrer geht im Zimmer auf und ab.
The teacher is going to and fro in the room.

When Georg Büchner's Woyzeck's mind begins to break, he imagines demonic rumblings about him and exclaims, *Es geht hinter mir, unter mir.* The important criterion for the accusative is that the motion must be directed to a place or goal. Kant's epitaph reads, *Das himmlische Gestirne über mir und das moralische Gesetz in mir.* (The heavenly constellations above me and the moral law within me.) There is no verb at all in the epitaph but the condition is clearly static.

Prepositions, because their meanings can vary so much depending on context, have been described as the "little devils" of language. The doubtful prepositions may seem especially devilish to you. They can, however, often express spatial relationships between things more precisely than is possible in English. The distinction between "in" and "into" exists in English also, but is not always made. In German this distinction is always made.

Er gießt das Wasser im Glas auf den Boden.
He's pouring the water in the glass onto the floor.

Er gießt das Wasser ins Glas.
He's pouring the water into the glass.

In the first instance, *in* + dative, the water is already in the glass and is being poured into or onto something else. In the second, *in* + accusative, the water is being poured from another container into the glass.

Another distinction in German concerns "to."

Wir gehen ins Theater.
We go to the theater. (a performance is attended)

Wir gehen zum Theater.
We go to the theater. (to the exterior of the building but not necessarily into it)

PITFALL

Unless one is actually on top of something, English "on" is not rendered by *auf* but by *an*. English songs are set "on" the Wabash, the Sewanee, the Mississippi, etc. In German one says:

Am Rhein, am herrlichen Rheine
On the Rhine, the splendid Rhine

An der Saale hellem Strande
On the bright shore of the Saale

An der Weser
On the Weser

Johann Strauss' famous waltz is entitled *An der schönen blauen Donau* which refers more to the ambience on the banks of the Danube than to anything on top of it. Of course, if you take a boat from Passau to Vienna or Budapest you would then say, *Wir fahren auf der Donau* (We travel on the Danube).

German uses *an* in translating Stratford-on-Avon, Hastings-on-Hudson, or Newcastle-on-Tyne.

Frankfurt am Main
Frankfurt on the Main

Frankfurt an der Oder
Frankfurt on the Oder

Marburg an der Lahn
Marburg on the Lahn

Auf + dative is sometimes translated "at."

Prepositional Idioms

RULE

Although prepositions have specific dictionary meanings, you must very often translate them with a different preposition in English, or even omit the preposition entirely.

---

an + dative

Er starb an einer schweren Krankheit.
He died of a severe illness.

Sie erkennt ihn an seinem Gang.
She recognizes him by his walk.

Sie rächten sich an ihren Feinden.
They took vengeance on their enemies.

Wollen Sie am Fest teilnehmen?
Do you want to participate in the celebration?

an + accusative

Sie glauben an viele Götter.
They believe in many gods.

Ich kann mich an seine Art nicht gewöhnen.
I can't get used to his ways.

Wir erinnern uns noch an ihn.
We still remember him.

Sie denkt noch an die schönen Stunden in Aranjuez.
She's still thinking of the lovely hours (spent) in Aranjuez.

Wir kommen zuerst an die Reihe.
It's our turn first.

aus + dative

Das Haus ist aus Holz.
The house is made of wood.

Was ist aus ihm geworden?
What has become of him?

für + accusative

Er hält sich für ein Genie.
He considers himself a genius.

Wir interessieren uns gar nicht dafür.
We're not at all interested in that.

in + accusative

Er verliebte sich in sie.
He fell in love with her.

gegen + accusative

Was kann man gegen eine Erkältung tun?
What can you do for a cold? (German usage is more logical.)

nach + dative

Iphigenie sehnt sich nach Griechenland.
Iphigenia is yearning for Greece.

Alles riecht nach Fisch.
Everything smells of fish.

Er strebt nach Ruhm.
He's striving for fame.

um + accusative

Ich bitte um Zeit.
I'm asking for time.

Er kämpfte um sein Leben.
He was fighting for his life.

Hat sie sich um die Stelle beworben?
Did she apply for the job?

Es handelt sich um viel Geld.
It's a matter of much money.

Es ist um uns geschehen.
It's all over with us. (We're done for.)

von + dative

Die Ratte lebte nur von Fett und Butter.
The rat lived only on fat and butter.

Wir halten nichts von dieser Sache.
We have a low opinion of this matter.

vor + dative

Hüte dich vor ihnen.
Beware of (Watch out for) them.

Sie erschrak vor dem Gespenst.
She was frightened by the ghost.

Er floh vor dem Mörder.
He fled from the murderer.

zu + dative

Ich gratuliere zum Geburtstag.
Congratulations on your birthday.

Man wählte ihn zum Präsidenten.
They elected him president.

Prepositional idioms are best learned with their verbs in specific constructions.
Auf and *über* always take the accusative when used figuratively.

Es kommt ganz auf Sie an.
It depends entirely on you.

Wir freuen uns auf die Ferien.
We're looking forward to vacation.

Warten Sie auf mich!
Wait for me.

Er sprach über die Liebe im klassischen Altertum.
He spoke of love in Classical Antiquity.

Karl der Große herrschte über viele Länder.
Charlemagne ruled over many lands.

RULE

To express "to think of" use *denken an* in German, except in reference to matters of opinion. In such cases use *denken von.*

Denkst du noch an ihn?
Are you still thinking of him?

Was denkst du von ihm?
What do you think of him? (opinion)

Both *denken von* and *denken über* can be used to express "to think about."

Was denken Sie davon? ⎫
Was denken Sie darüber? ⎭   What do you think about it?

RULE

When several prepositions are used in a series, the case of the word following is determined by the last preposition.

Das Göttliche existiert in, mit, um, und durch alle Dinge und Kreaturen.
The divine exists in, with, around, and through all things and creatures.

RULE

The so-called Saxon Genitive, used in poetry, proverbs, and older literature, intervenes between the preposition and the noun it governs.

Durch der Glieder angespannte Stille (Rilke)
Through the tense silence of the limbs

Durch der Blätter dunkle Hülle (Henckell)
Through the dark veil of the leaves

Mit der Liebe holden Schranken (Goethe)
With the gentle bonds of love

In des Lebens Frühlingstagen (Beethoven's *Fidelio*)
In the springtime of life

In ordinary, everyday German, these would read as follows:

Durch die angespannte Stille der Glieder

Durch die dunkle Hülle der Blätter

Mit den holden Schranken der Liebe

In den Frühlingstagen des Lebens

RULE

The prepositions *(an)statt, ohne,* and *um* can introduce an infinitival phrase. The translation of *(an)statt* and *ohne* calls for an English gerund (*-ing*). Case is determined by use in the sentence, not by the preposition.

Anstatt seinen Freuden zu helfen, dachte er nur an sich.
Instead of helping his friends, he thought only of himself.

Ohne ihm die Hand zu reichen, verließ sie das Zimmer.
Without shaking hands with him, she left the room.

Um auf diesem Gebiete weitere Fortschritte zu machen . . .
(In order) to make further progress in this field . . .

RULE

In written and spoken German it is very common to contract prepositions with a following definite article. **No apostrophe is used.**

---

with *den:* hintern, übern, untern.

with *das:* ans, aufs, durchs, fürs, hinters, ins, übers, ums, unters, vors.

with *dem:* am, außerm, beim, hinterm, im, überm, unterm, vom, vorm, zum.

with *der* (feminine dative): zur.

PITFALL

Some prepositional contractions are colloquial and an apostrophe *is* used with them. These are common in spoken German but should not be used in writing.

an'n	for an den	für'n	for für den
auf'n	for auf den	gegen's	for gegen das
auf'm	for auf dem	in'n	for in den
aus'm	for aus dem	nach'm	for nach dem

There are additional colloquial contractions, many of which are dialect forms.

6 ■ Pronouns

PRONOUNS

A pronoun is a word that stands for a noun.

RULE

A pronoun can refer to a word, idea, person, or thing. Thus a pronoun has an antecedent to which it refers. If the pronoun is interrogative (who?, which?, what?), the speaker is asking for the identity of the antecedent.

Personal Pronouns

Singular

Nom. ich (I)	du (you)	er, sie, es (he, she, it)
Gen. meiner (of me)	deiner (of you)	seiner, ihrer, seiner (of him, her, it)
Dat. mir (to me)	dir (to you)	ihm, ihr, ihm (to him, her, it)
Acc. mich (me)	dich (you)	ihn, sie, es (him, her, it)

Plural

Nom. wir (we)	ihr (you)	sie, Sie (they, you)
Gen. unser (of us)	euer (of you)	ihrer, Ihrer (of them, you)
Dat. uns (to us)	euch (to you)	ihnen, Ihnen (to them, you)
Acc. uns (us)	euch (you)	sie, Sie (them, you)

PITFALL

Modern English has only the one word "you." In German there are three ways to say "you." Be careful not to confuse them.

The familiar or *du-* form is used when talking to a child, relative, close friend, animal, the deity, or an inanimate object, for example, Wolfram von Eschenbach's famous address to the evening star (*O du mein holder Abendstern*) in Wagner's *Tannhäuser.*

The *ihr-* form is the plural of *du* and is used to address friends, relatives, children, animals, inanimate objects, and deities.

The polite or formal *Sie* is used in all other instances, sometimes even to friends and associates to show respect.

The "thou" form is no longer part of the living language in English. In poetry, "thou" survived into the early twentieth century. But unlike its etymological equivalent in English ("thou"), German *du* is a frequently used part of everyday speech.

There is a tendency among young people to avoid the formal *Sie* when addressing each other, even if they have just met. Nevertheless, you should not use *du* to a person with whom you are not familiar. A woman should not use *du* to a man she doesn't know well, although she may, of course, deliberately use the *du* form to him, if she cares to. Harry Haller in Hesse's *Steppenwolf* is addressed in the *du-* form by a girl (Hermine) he doesn't know. When he replies stiffly in the *Sie-* form, she scolds him for being "square." The Germans have their problems with *du* and *Sie*. At parties they may get chummy and use the familiar *du,* but when they meet later they're often uncomfortable with it and want to revert to *Sie* or resort to impersonal circumlocutions. This has been satirized in Johann Strauss' *Die Fledermaus* when the guests at Prince Orlofsky's party regale themselves with champagne and familiarity:

> **Laßt das traute Du uns schenken,**
> **Für die Ewigkeit**
> **Immer so, wie heut',**
> **Wenn wir morgen noch dran denken!**
> **Erst ein Kuß, dann ein Du,**
> **Du, Du, Du, immerzu!**

A very free translation is "Let's buddy up forever, eternally, perhaps we'll still remember it tomorrow. First a kiss, then a *Du*, on and on." The ritual is sometimes called *Bruderschaft trinken.*

Another problem is when to stop using *du* to a child. This is usually done around the age of sixteen, although there is no fixed age for the transition to *Sie.*

PITFALL

The word *sie* can have several meanings. Although German is a far more inflected language than English, in the case of *sie,* English distinguishes between subject and object and German does not.

Nom.   sie (she, they)

Acc.   sie (her, them)

Mark Twain, in his essay "The Awful German Language" in *A Tramp Abroad,* complains about *sie,* "...the poor little weak thing of only three letters having to do the work of six (words)." However, because of the verb endings it is not difficult to distinguish between:

Sie tanzt.	*and*	**Sie tanzen.**
She dances.		They (you) dance.
Sie wird tanzen.		**Sie werden tanzen.**
She will dance.		They (you) will dance.
Sie hat getanzt.		**Sie haben getanzt.**
She has danced.		They (you) have danced.

In written German it is possible to distinguish between *sie* meaning "they" and *Sie* meaning "you," since *sie* (they) is not capitalized, except at the beginning of a sentence. Forms of the definite article *die* can be substituted for *sie* to avoid ambiguity. (See Articles, p.24.)

Wo arbeiten die?
Where do they work?

Was wollen die?
What do they want?

PITFALL

The word *ihr* can have several meanings. Do not confuse pronouns with the possessive adjective *ihr.*

Ich schreibe ihr einen Brief.
I'm writing a letter to her.
(*ihr* is used here as the dative of the pronoun *sie*)

Wenn ihr wollt, kommt morgen.
If you want, come tomorrow.
(*ihr* is used here as the second person plural personal pronoun)

Sie hat ihren Brief schon geschrieben.
She's already written her letter.
(*ihr* is used here as a possessive adjective)

Agreement of Pronoun

RULE

The word "it" in English does not automatically mean *es* in German. German nouns, and the pronouns for which they stand, can be masculine, feminine, or neuter. *Es* means "it" only when referring to neuter nouns.

Der Baum ist hoch.	**Er ist hoch.**
The tree is high.	It is high.
Sehen Sie den Baum?	**Ich sehe ihn noch nicht.**
Do you see the tree?	I don't see it yet.
Wo haben Sie die Uhr gekauft?	**Ich habe sie gefunden.**
Where did you buy the watch?	I found it.
Er möchte das Haus kaufen.	**Er möchte es kaufen.**
He'd like to buy the house.	He'd like to buy it.

RULE

Grammatical gender is used for the pronoun in the case of nouns with a fixed gender or nouns used for both male and female beings.
(See Nouns, p. 47.)

Der Dienstbote und die Schildwache bekamen ein Kind.
The servant and the sentry had a child.

Er war eine gute Mutter und sie war ein guter Vater.
She was a good mother and he was a good father.

PITFALL

In the case of neuter nouns ending in *-chen* or *-lein*, practice varies. Sometimes the grammatical gender *es* is used (especially in formal writing), sometimes the logical gender, *er* or *sie*.

Was macht Ihr Söhnchen?
What's your little boy doing?
Es (or Er) geht schon in die Schule.
He's already going to school.

Das Mädchen will nicht mehr tanzen.
The girl doesn't want to dance any more.
Es (or Sie) ist müde.
She is tired.

Use of the logical gender is more colloquial.

PITFALL

Es can be used as an introductory subject even though the real subject is a noun. Whether the verb is singular or plural will depend on the real subject. This construction is widely used in German to give greater emphasis to the real subject. Sometimes it is translated by "there" in English.

Es ging ein alter Mann die Straße hinunter.
There was an old man going down the street.

Es bellen die Hunde.
The dogs are barking.

Es ruhen die Wälder.
The forests are at rest.

Es schläft die ganze Welt.
The whole world is sleeping.

Es klirrten die Becher, es jauchzten die Knecht' (Heine)
The goblets clinked, the henchmen jubilated

RULE

The indefinite pronoun *man* takes third person singular verb endings, like the English "one." It can only be used in the nominative and thus always is the subject.

For the other cases, forms of *ein-* are used. *Einer* also exists in the nominative but *man* is more common. *Man* is frequently translated by "you" (in American English) or "people," or by a passive, or the indefinite "they." The possessive adjective used with *man* is *sein*.

Man kann dort sehr gut essen.
One can eat very well there.

Man hat es mir versprochen.
They promised it to me. (It was promised to me.)

Es freut einen, so etwas anzusehen.
It pleases one to look at something like that.

Man soll seine Arbeit tun und andere in Ruhe lassen.
One should do one's work and leave others alone.
(People should do their work and leave others alone.)

PITFALL

Do not confuse the indefinite pronoun *man* with the noun *der Mann* or with the colloquial North German adverb *man*.

Geh man die Straße hinunter. (Borchert)
Just walk down the street.

Geh du man vor!
Just go on ahead.

Die hat's man eilig.
She's in quite a hurry.

PITFALL

When *ein-* words are used as pronouns they have the complete inflectional endings of the *der-* words. Thus you must be careful of the masculine nominative and the neuter nominative and accusative. *Ein-* words have no endings in these forms when used as adjectives but have *der-* word endings when used as pronouns.

Dort liegt sein Mantel. Wo ist meiner?
His coat is over there. Where is mine?

Hier ist sein Buch. Wo ist deines?
Here is his book. Where is yours?

Reflexive Pronouns

Reflexive pronouns in German are the same as personal pronouns except in the third person singular and plural where *sich* is used for both the dative and the accusative.

RULE

To indicate that a verb is reflexive, *sich* is placed before the infinitive: *sich setzen, sich waschen,* etc.

PITFALL

Although the third person form *sich* does not distinguish between dative and accusative, the first and second person singular forms do (*mir* and *mich; dir* and *dich*).

Ich wasche mich.
I wash myself.

Ich kaufe mir eine neue Krawatte.
I buy myself a new tie.

PITFALL

The use of the reflexive is much more frequent in German than in English. The reflexive cannot be omitted as in English.

Er rasiert sich jeden Morgen.
He shaves every morning.

Er hat sich nicht gebadet.
He didn't bathe.

Overuse of the reflexive in English is a bit folksy or rural.

I want to buy myself a new watch.
Ich will mir eine neue Uhr kaufen.

She wants to pick herself out a nice dress.
Sie will sich ein schönes Kleid aussuchen.

PITFALL

Many verbs are reflexive in German but not in English. Most of them take the accusative.

Er interessiert sich dafür.
He's interested in that.

Sie hat sich erkältet.
She caught cold.

Setzen Sie sich!
Sit down!

Ich freue mich darüber.
I'm glad about it.

Er ärgerte sich darüber.
He was angry about it.

PITFALL

Do not confuse the intensifier *selbst* (or *selber*) with a reflexive pronoun. *Selbst* is never declined, i.e., it always stays the same. *Selbst* can never substitute for a reflexive.

Das Kind wäscht sich selbst.
The child washes himself.

Selbst has been added to indicate that another person no longer washes the child but that he washes by himself.

Note: When *selbst* precedes a noun, it means "even." When it comes after, it means "self."

Selbst Oma hat es gemacht.
Even Granny did it.

| **Oma selbst hat es gemacht.**
Granny herself made it.

Relative Pronouns

RULE

A relative pronoun relates or refers to another pronoun or a noun (its antecedent) with which it must agree in gender and number.

	Masc.	Fem.	Neuter	Plural (all genders)
Nom.	der	die	das	die
Gen.	dessen	deren	dessen	deren
Dat.	dem	der	dem	denen
Acc.	den	die	das	die

Forms of *welcher* may be substituted for the above (except in the genitive) but the most common relatives are *der, die, das*. *Welcher* forms are used today chiefly to avoid repeating *das*.

Dieses Haus, welches das schönste im Dorf ist, . . .
This house, which is the most beautiful in the village, . . .

| PITFALL

Although the relative pronoun is essentially the same as the definite article, the four genitive forms *dessen, deren, dessen, deren* and the dative plural *denen* differ.

Der Junge, dessen Eltern gestorben sind, ist jetzt im Waisenhaus.
The boy whose parents died is now in the orphanage.

Die Kleine, deren Eltern gestorben sind, ist jetzt im Waisenhaus.
The little girl whose parents died is now in the orphanage.

Das Kind, dessen Eltern gestorben sind, ist jetzt im Waisenhaus.
The child whose parents died is now in the orphanage.

Die Kinder, deren Eltern gestorben sind, sind jetzt im Waisenhaus.
The children whose parents died are now in the orphanage.

PITFALL

In expressing the genitive "whose," be sure to remember whether the antecedent is masculine, feminine, or neuter. See the examples given in the preceding pitfall. Do not be misled by the gender of the noun following the relative pronoun but refer to the antecedent.

Das ist der Maler, mit dessen Mutter er bekannt ist.
That's the painter whose mother he knows.

Although *Mutter* is feminine, "whose" refers to *der Maler*. Similarly:

Das ist die Malerin, mit deren Vater er bekannt ist.
That's the painter (female) with whose father he is acquainted.

PITFALL

Although the relative pronoun, like other pronouns, agrees with its antecedent in gender and number, its case depends on the construction of its own clause.

Der Baum, der im Garten steht, . . .
The tree which is in the garden, . . .

Der Baum, dessen Blätter jetzt rot sind, . . .
The tree whose leaves are now red, . . .

Der Baum, von dem Claudel spricht, . . .
The tree of which Claudel speaks, . . .

Der Baum, den Susanne gezeichnet hat, . . .
The tree which Susanne drew, . . .

RULE

Every relative clause is a subordinate clause, i.e., the finite (conjugated or personal) verb is placed at the end of that clause.

See sections on Conjunctions and Word Order and Sentence Structure, p. 36 and p. 147. Like all other dependent clauses, relative clauses are set off by commas.

Der Zug, mit dem wir nach Italien gefahren sind, war sehr lang.

The train by which we traveled to Italy was very long.

Die Straße, in der er wohnt, ist sehr elegant.

The street on which he lives is very elegant.

Das Haus, das wir uns gekauft haben, ist wunderschön gelegen.

The house which we bought is beautifully situated.

RULE

German must use a relative clause in constructions where English places a present participle after a noun.

---

the people dancing
die Leute, die tanzen

the lady singing
die Frau, die singt

the man sitting over there
der Mann, der dort drüben sitzt

the boy playing in the garden
der Junge, der im Garten spielt

RULE

English frequently omits the relative pronoun. This can *never* be done in German.

The books (which, that) I bought yesterday are interesting.
Die Bücher, die ich gestern gekauft habe, sind interessant.

That's the girl (whom, that) I saw there.
Das ist das Mädchen, das ich dort gesehen habe.

The train (which, that) they want to take doesn't stop there.
Der Zug, den sie nehmen wollen, hält dort nicht.

RULE

English frequently uses "that" as a relative pronoun. It can be translated by German *das* only when it refers to a neuter noun in the nominative or accusative.

Das ist das Mädchen, das er geheiratet hat.
That's the girl (whom, that) he married.

In all other instances the relative pronoun must agree in gender and number with its antecedent.

Das ist der Mann, den sie geheiratet hat.
That's the man (whom, that) she married.

Sehen Sie die Kinder, die im Garten spielen?
Do you see the children (that, who are) playing in the garden?

Note: German *das,* like English "that," can be used as an indefinite relative pronoun and refer to an entire idea.

Sie liebt dich sehr.   **Das weiß ich.**
She loves you very much.   I know that.

Die Erde ist rund.   **Das glaube ich nicht.**
The earth is round.   I don't believe that.

Interrogative Pronouns and Adjectives

Interrogative pronouns are used to ask questions.

Nom.	**wer** (who?)
Gen.	**wessen** (whose?)
Dat.	**wem** (to whom?)
Acc.	**wen** (whom?)

RULE

English "who" is both relative and interrogative. Except for placing a question mark after direct questions, English does not distinguish between the interrogative and relative use of "who, whose, whom." German does make the distinction.

Interrogative

Wer ist hier?
Who is here?

Wessen Haus ist dies?
Whose house is this?

Mit wem sprechen Sie?
With whom are you speaking?

Wen haben Sie dort gesehen?
Whom did you see there?

Relative

Der Junge, der dort steht, ist mein Freund.
The boy who is standing there is my friend.

Er ist der Junge, dessen Mutter gestorben ist.
He is the boy whose mother died.

Das ist die Frau, mit der ich gesprochen habe.
That's the lady with whom I spoke.

Das ist das Mädchen, das ich dort gesehen habe.
That's the girl whom I saw there.

RULE

No distinction is made in German between gender and number in the interrogative pronouns. The relative pronouns, however, must show these distinctions.

Interrogative

Wer ist dieser Mann?
Who is this man?

Wer ist diese Frau?
Who is this woman?

Wer ist dieses Kind?	**Wer sind diese Männer? (Frauen, Kinder)**
Who is this child?	Who are these men? (women, children)

Relative

Der Mann, der dort sitzt, ist mein Onkel.
The man who is sitting there is my uncle.

Die Frau, die das getan hat, verdient größte Achtung.
The lady who did that deserves the greatest respect.

Das Kind, das dort spielt, ist sehr schmutzig.
The child who is playing there is very dirty.

Die Männer, die jetzt tanzen, sind meine Freunde.
The men who are dancing now are my friends.

This absence of plural and feminine forms in the interrogative pronouns is the subject of a humorous poem by Christian Morgenstern. The poem relates how a *Werwolf* (werewolf) turns to a dead *Dorfschulmeister* (village schoolmaster) with the request to decline him (*Bitte, beuge mich!*). The schoolmaster obliges but has to disappoint the werewolf in that there is no plural to *Werwolf* (". . . 'wer' gäbs nur im Singular.").

PITFALL

Occasionally *wer* can also be used as a relative pronoun. In such cases it always refers to somebody indefinite and is often used in proverbs and general statements. It corresponds to English "who, whoever, he who."

Wer sich nicht selbst befiehlt,/Bleibt immer ein Knecht.
(Goethe)
Whoever doesn't command himself is forever a slave.

Wer nicht für mich ist, ist gegen mich.
He who is not for me is against me.

RULE

English "what?" is not always *was* in German. *Was* cannot be used interrogatively before a noun. Forms of *welcher* must be used instead.

Welches Buch haben Sie gewählt?
What book did you choose?

Mit welchem Zug sind Sie gefahren?
With what train did you travel?

Aus welchem Werk haben Sie das zitiert?
From what work did you quote that?

RULE

After neuter adjectives and pronouns and after indefinites like *alles, nichts,* and *etwas,* German uses the relative *was,* not *das.*

English usually omits the relative but sometimes uses "that." In German, *was* cannot be omitted.

Das ist alles, was ich weiß.
That is all (that) I know.

Er hat nichts, was ich will.
He has nothing (that) I want.

Wir brauchen etwas, was nur Sie uns geben können.
We need something (that) only you can give us.

After superlatives, *was* is similarly used:

Das ist das Schönste, was ich je gesehen habe.
That's the most beautiful thing (that) I've ever seen.

When *was* refers to an entire preceding idea it translates as "which" or "as."

Die Liebe macht blind, was jeder weiß.
Love makes blind, which (as) everybody knows.

Sie sind spät nach Hause gekommen, was mir gar nicht gefallen hat.
They came home late, which didn't please me at all.

Er hat die Arbeit noch nicht erledigt, was mich sehr stört.
He hasn't done the job yet, which disturbs me a lot.

Prepositional Compounds Used Pronominally

Wo and *da* are frequently combined with prepositions. Mark Twain once remarked that he loved the word *damit* until he found out what it meant.

Similar compounds with "where" and "there" exist in English but they occur primarily in older literature, for example, Juliet's question, "Wherefore art thou Romeo?" and in legal language. Today few other than lawyers would use "whereas, wherein, whereby, whereupon, whereafter," etc. The same forms exist with "there," as in "thereby, thereupon," etc. Do not use them in translating German *worin*, *darin*, etc. Nevertheless, being aware of the literal translation will help you in vocabulary building and comprehension. In German, prepositional compounds are quite natural and a part of everyday language. If one translates them literally, the similarity to English is obvious, but in the more usual translation the words are reversed.

Ich weiß, wovon ich spreche.
I know what I'm talking about.
(I know whereof I speak.)

Was soll ich damit machen?
What should I do with it?
(What should I do therewith?)

Ich habe nichts dagegen.
I have nothing against it.

RULE

  Da and *wo* compounds are used only for inanimate objects and cannot be used for people. Use a pronoun instead when dealing with people.

Womit schreibt er?
With what is he writing?

Er schreibt mit einem Bleistift.   Er schreibt damit.
He's writing with a pencil.   He's writing with it.

Worüber schreibt er?   Über moderne Malerei.
What's he writing about? About modern painting.

Ich wußte nicht, daß er darüber schreibt.
I didn't know that he's writing about it.

Wovon erzählten sie? — Von der Reise.   Sie erzählten davon.
                                            They talked about
What did they speak of? — Of the trip.   it.

But:

Mit wem geht er?	**Er geht mit seinem Freund.**
With whom is he going?	He's going with his friend.
Er geht mit ihm.	
He's going with him.	
Mit wem spricht er?	**Er spricht mit seiner Geliebten.**
With whom is he talking?	He's talking with his beloved.
Er spricht mit ihr.	
He's talking with her.	

RULE

In prepositional questions referring to inanimate objects, a *wo*-phrase must be used instead of *was*.

Woran glaubst du?
What do you believe in?

Wovon sprechen Sie?
What are you talking about?

Womit schreiben Sie?
With what are you writing?

7 ■ Verbs

VERBS

Verbs denote actions or states of being. They have tenses (time indications), voices (active or passive), and moods (indicative or subjunctive). German and English verbs are divided into two basic groups, weak (regular) and strong (irregular) verbs.

Principal Parts of Strong and Weak Verbs

It is important that you memorize the principal parts of strong verbs. They are called *strong* because a vowel change does the work of indicating the change from present to past time. Weak verbs are much easier to learn because there is no vowel change, and because the first and third person singular of the past tense always end in *-te,* and their past participles always end in *-t*. Most English and German verbs are weak, i.e., they do not change their stem vowel but merely add a suffix to form the past tense. In English this suffix is *-ed*. In German it is *-te.*

> **lieben** (to love)   **liebte** (loved)   **geliebt** (loved)

Principal parts of common strong verbs, arranged according to pattern of change, will be found at the end of this chapter. It is best to learn principal parts of each strong verb as you meet it. Sometimes grammars and dictionaries use a kind of shorthand to indicate principal parts, for example:

> **graben**—(to dig) u, a, ä

This translates as: **graben, grub, gegraben, gräbt**
                     to dig, dug, dug,   digs

In some texts the third person singular of the present tense is given, often in parentheses, immediately after the infinitive. Other texts omit this third person singular present tense form entirely, except for those verbs whose stem vowel changes. (See Vowel Changes in the Present Tense and *Du*- Imperative of Strong Verbs, later in this chapter, p. 103.)

> PITFALL
>
> Do not assume that a verb is strong simply because its infinitive resembles other strong verbs. *Tragen* and *schlagen*, for instance, follow the pattern of *graben* given above.
>
> **tragen, trug, getragen, trägt**
> **schlagen, schlug, geschlagen, schlägt**
>
> But verbs such as *sagen*, *klagen*, and *fragen* are weak.
>
> **sagen, sagte, gesagt, sagt**
> **klagen, klagte, geklagt, klagt**
>
> Learn the principal parts of each strong verb as you meet it.

Verb Tenses

Tense means *time*. It is very important to keep the tenses and their endings straight, although it may make you tense to do so!

THE PRESENT TENSE

> RULE
>
> This tense, for both weak and strong verbs, is formed by removing the sign of the infinitive *-en* to get the verb stem and then adding the endings *-e*, *-st*, *-t* in the singular, and *-en*, *-t*, *-en* in the plural. Verbs whose stems end in *-d*, *-t* or *-n* preceded by a consonant insert an *-e* between the stem and the ending *-t* or *-st* to facilitate pronunciation, for example, *du arbeitest, er findet.*

As in English, the personal pronouns are usually not omitted. You must memorize the present tense endings. It would be as serious a mistake in German to say *wir geht* as *"we goes"* would be in English. Present tense endings can be added to foreign words to create German verbs, of a sort. In the seventeenth century, Germans did this to French words and came up with forms like *ich chantiere* and *wir parlieren*. German-Americans do this with English verbs. H.L. Mencken once facetiously contemplated doing a German-American grammar. He offered the conjugation of the nonexistent *leiken* "to like": *ich leike, du leikst, er leikt; wir leiken, ihr leikt, sie leiken.*

Both English and German can use the present with a future implication; however, this usage is more common in German.

Ich bleibe zwei Tage in Frankfurt, dann fahre ich nach Stuttgart.
I'll stay in Frankfurt for two days; then I'll go to Stuttgart.

Er bringt es nächste Woche.
He'll bring it next week.

PITFALL

Do not use forms of *tun* or *sein* to translate English emphatic and progressive forms of the present or past. In German *sein* forms do not exist, and forms with *tun* are dialect or incorrect.

Sie sprechen Deutsch.
You speak German. (You are speaking German. You do speak German.)

PITFALL

It is similarly wrong to use *tun* or *sein* in questions or negative statements. In modern English only the verbs "to have" and "to be" can be inverted to form questions:

Is he here?   Has he time for that?
Ist er hier?   **Hat er Zeit dafür?**

In German, however, all verbs invert to form questions:

Tanzt er mit Anna?
Is he dancing with Anna?

Wissen Sie die Antwort?
Do you know the answer?

RULE
The German present tense is used in time expressions for actions that began in the past and continue into the present. Often *schon* (already) or *seit* (since), or both, are used in such constructions.

Ich bin schon seit zwanzig Jahren in Amerika.
I have already been in America for twenty years.

Wir warten schon zwei Stunden.
We've already been waiting for two hours.

VOWEL CHANGES IN THE PRESENT TENSE AND *DU-* IMPERATIVE OF STRONG VERBS

RULE

Weak verbs never change their stem vowel but many strong verbs change it in the second and third person singular of the present tense and in the *du-* imperative.

Check list of principal parts, p. 142.

Change from e to i

Strong verbs like *geben, helfen, treffen* change *e* to *i* in the forms *du gibst, er gibt,* and *gib! Werden* belongs in this category but the *du-* imperative does not change.

Mensch, werde wesentlich! (Angelus Silesius)
Man, become (be) existential.

Werde kalt und hart wie du kannst! (Wagner's Siegfried to his sword)
Become cold and hard as you can!

Change from e to ie

Befehlen, empfehlen, and *lesen* have *ie* in the second and third person singular and in the *du-* imperative.

ich befehle	wir befehlen
du bef*ie*hlst	ihr befehlt
er bef*ie*hlt	sie befehlen

The *du-* imperative is bef*ie*hl!

Change from a to ä and au to äu

Verbs like *fallen, lassen, tragen, laufen,* and *saufen* add an umlaut in the *du* and *er* forms of the present tense but do not do so in the *du-* imperative.

ich trage	wir tragen
du trägst	ihr tragt
er trägt	sie tragen

The *du-* imperative is *trage!*, or more colloquially, *trag!* There is no umlaut. The same pattern is observed with *laufen*.

ich laufe	wir laufen
du läufst	ihr lauft
er läuft	sie laufen

Du- imperative: *laufe!* (*lauf!*)

PAST TENSE (IMPERFECT)

> **RULE**
>
> Weak verbs add the endings *-te, -test, -te* in the singular and *-ten, -tet, -ten* in the plural. These endings are added to the stem, i.e., the infinitive without *-en*.

ich hoffte	wir hofften
du hofftest	ihr hofftet
er hoffte	sie hofften

Strong verbs have no ending in the first and third persons singular. The second person singular ending is *-st* and the plural endings are *-en, -t, -en*.

ich trank	wir tranken
du trankst	ihr trankt
er trank	sie tranken

> **RULE**
>
> Do not add an ending to the third person singular of the past tense.

The first and third persons singular of weak verbs *both* end in *-te*, whereas the first and third persons singular of strong verbs have no ending.

Weak	*Strong*
er sagte	er ging
he said	he went
sie spielte	sie fuhr
she played	she drove

Since students usually spend a lot of time on the present tense and master those endings, they tend to put a -*t* (present tense ending) on third person singular past forms also. This mistake is similar to adding an English present tense -*s* ending to the past tense. Despite the similarity of many present and past tense endings, remember that the third person singular past tense in German never ends in -*t*. This is true of both weak and strong verbs.

Do not confuse weak and strong verbs by adding the weak endings in -*te* to the past of strong verbs. This would be comparable to saying he "sanged" or I "wented" in English.

PITFALL

A group of nine verbs known as irregular mixed verbs and *wissen,* does, however, do just that. They are called *mixed* because they have characteristics of both weak and strong verbs. Like weak verbs, they add -*te* endings to their past tense, and their past participles end in -*t*. However, like strong verbs, they change the stem vowel of the infinitive in the past tense and in the past participle.

Infinitive	Past (Imperfect)	Past Participle
brennen (to burn)	brannte	gebrannt
bringen (to bring)	brachte	gebracht
denken (to think)	dachte	gedacht
kennen (to know)	kannte	gekannt
nennen (to name)	nannte	genannt
rennen (to run)	rannte	gerannt
senden (to send)	sandte	gesandt
wenden (to turn)	wandte	gewandt
wissen (to know)	wußte	gewußt

Note: The weak forms, *sendete, gesendet* and *wendete, gewendet* are also found, primarily in poetry and older literature. In the meaning "to broadcast by radio or TV," the weak forms, *sendete, gesendet* must be used.

PRESENT PERFECT TENSE

Both German and English use the past participle with a helping verb (called "auxiliary verb") to form the perfect tenses. The term "perfect" comes from the Latin and means "finished, done." It refers to the past participle. Every perfect tense, in English and in German, has a past participle and this past participle never changes.

RULE

A perfect tense cannot be used, in either language, without an "auxiliary" verb—"to have" in English, and either *haben* or *sein* in German.

There are several differences in German and English usage of the perfect tenses as the following pitfalls will point out.

PITFALL

Unlike English, the past participle in German is placed at the end of a sentence or clause, *unless* the clause is a subordinate clause. Then the auxiliary verb is the last word. (See chapters on "Conjunctions" and "Word Order and Sentence Structure" p. 36 and 147.)

Ich hab mein Herz in San Francisco gelassen.
I left my heart in San Francisco.

Ich hab mein Herz in Heidelberg verloren.
I lost my heart in Heidelberg.

But if this expression of romantic attachment to San Francisco and Heidelberg in the two popular songs had occurred in a subordinate clause, the auxiliary verb would be last. (For a discussion of subordinate clauses, see the chapters on "Conjunctions" and "Word Order and Sentence Structure," pp. 36 and 147.)

Ich bin traurig, weil ich mein Herz in San Francisco gelassen habe.
I'm sad because I left my heart in San Francisco.

Ich sage, daß ich mein Herz in Heidelberg verloren habe.
I say that I've lost my heart in Heidelberg.

PITFALL

Most German past participles begin with *ge-*. English stopped using the prefix centuries ago. Inseparable prefix verbs and the many *-ieren* verbs have no *ge-* in the past participle.

Wir haben die Arbeit gründlich besprochen.
We discussed the work thoroughly.

Sie hat nichts probiert und nichts riskiert.
She tried nothing and risked nothing.

Note: Unlike most *-ieren* verbs, *schmieren* and *frieren* are of Germanic origin. Their past participles are therefore *geschmiert* and *gefroren.*

PITFALL

Except for the *mixed* verbs previously mentioned, all strong verbs have a past participle ending in *-en.* The past participle of weak verbs ends in *-t.* Do not confuse them. Forms such as *gegangt* and *gesungt* are as wrong as "wented" and "sanged" are in English.

PITFALL

It is very often necessary to translate a German present perfect by using an English past.

Haydn hat viele Symphonien komponiert.
Haydn wrote many symphonies.

Ich habe ihn gestern in der Stadt gesehen.
I saw him yesterday in town.

Goethe und Schiller haben einander viele Briefe geschrieben.
Goethe and Schiller wrote many letters to each other.

> The present perfect is the usual past tense in conversation. The imperfect (past) is used for a connected narrative, or events in sequence.
>
> **Er kam nach Hause, beschimpfte seine Frau, aß zu Abend, las die Zeitung, trank sein Bier, und schlief beim Fernsehen ein.**
> He came home, bawled out his wife, ate dinner, read the newspaper, drank his beer, and fell asleep watching television.

RULE

English and German past participles, when used as verbs, can never be used alone. They must have an auxiliary verb.

Was Sie getan haben, habe ich gesehen.
I saw what you did. (Not "seen" and "done," unless one says "I have seen what you have done.")

It is actually a worse mistake in English than in German, since the past participle occasionally occurs alone (mainly in literary usages) in German.

Past participles may be used as adjectives and are then treated like any other adjective, i.e., they can have endings. (See Adjectives, p. 1.)

der zerbrochene Krug	**die zerbrochenen Krüge**
the broken jug	the broken jugs
ein zerbrochener Krug	**zerbrochene Krüge**
a broken jug	broken jugs

SEIN- VERBS

RULE

Most German verbs use *haben* as the auxiliary in the perfect tenses. But intransitive verbs, i.e., verbs which do not take a direct object, are conjugated with *sein*.

---

aufstehen (to get up)	**fliegen** (to fly)
begegnen (to meet)	**fliehen** (to flee)
bleiben (to remain)	**folgen** (to follow)
fahren (to travel)	**gehen** (to go)
fallen (to fall)	**geschehen** (to happen)

gleiten (to glide)   springen (to jump)
kommen (to come)   steigen (to climb)
laufen (to run)   sterben (to die)
reisen (to travel)   treten (to step)
schleichen (to sneak)   wandern (to wander, hike)
schreiten (to step)   weichen (to yield)
schwimmen (to swim)   werden (to become)
sein (to be)

These verbs are intransitive, and except for *sein* and *bleiben,* express motion or a change of condition. They often require a prepositional phrase to complete their meaning. Verbs conjugated with "to be" are no longer in use in English although examples abound in the King James Bible and in Shakespeare, for example, "Toward Peloponnesus are they fled." (*Antony and Cleopatra*) Occasionally, even twentieth-century authors use them for literary effect, for example, "He was become wise in the ways of the club." (Jack London, *Call of the Wild*)

PITFALL

Sein- verbs can take *haben* if used transitively, i.e., if they take a direct object (accusative case), or an accusative of definite time.

Without a direct object:
Er ist im See geschwommen.
He swam in the lake.
Er ist nach Hause gefahren.
He drove home.

With a direct object or accusative of time:
Er hat eine halbe Stunde geschwommen.
He swam (for) a half hour.
Er hat mich nach Hause gefahren.
He drove me home.

PITFALL

Not all compounds of a prefix plus *kommen, fallen, steigen* or any other *sein-* verb necessarily use *sein* as the auxiliary in the perfect tenses. It depends in each case on whether the verb is intransitive and expresses motion or change of condition. If so, the auxiliary used is *sein.* The prefix *be-* often serves to make intransitive verbs transitive.

Er ist gestern gekommen.
He came yesterdáy.

But:

Er hat gestern einen Brief bekommen.
He received a letter yesterday.

PITFALL

For verbs which use *sein* in the perfect tenses (*sein*- verbs) remember to use *war* for English "had" in the past perfect and *sein* for "have" in the future perfect.

Sie waren zu früh abgereist.
They had left too early.

Sie werden zu früh abgereist sein.
They will have left too early.

FUTURE AND FUTURE PERFECT TENSES

RULE

The **future** is formed with the present tense of *werden* and the infinitive of the main verb. The **future perfect** also uses the present tense of *werden* but with a perfect infinitive. A perfect infinitive consists of the past participle of the main verb and the auxiliary *haben* or *sein*.

The future perfect is not frequently used. In colloquial speech the present is often used with a future implication. (See Present Tense in this chapter, p. 102.) As in English the auxiliary (*werden*) is used only once no matter how many infinitives follow.

Future
Sie wird tanzen, lachen und Rotwein trinken.
She will dance, laugh, and drink red wine.

Future Perfect
Sie wird getanzt, gelacht und Rotwein getrunken haben.
She will have danced, laughed, and drunk red wine.
(*Or:* She probably danced, laughed, and drank red wine.)

PITFALL

In German there is only one auxiliary, the present tense of *wer-*

den for all persons in the future tense. English may use "shall" or "will." German does not use *wollen* or *sollen*.

Ich werde tanzen.
I shall (will) dance.

Er wird tanzen.
He will (shall) dance.

PITFALL

The infinitive of the main verb is used without *zu* and is placed at the end of the clause or sentence. In subordinate clauses, however, the forms of *werden* occur last.

Ich werde die ganze Nacht mit ihr tanzen.
I'll dance all night with her.

Wann wirst du deinen Roman schreiben?
When will you write your novel?

But in subordinate clauses:

Ich weiß nicht, ob ich mit ihr tanzen werde.
I don't know if I'll dance with her.

Ich hoffe, daß ich ihn bald schreiben werde.
I hope that I'll write it soon.

PITFALL

The future is also used to express present probability. The adverb *wohl* frequently accompanies this usage.

Der Hund wird wohl sieben Jahre alt sein.
The dog is probably seven years old.

Er wird wohl jetzt zufrieden sein.
He's probably satisfied now.

PITFALL

The future perfect, an infrequently used tense, can similarly express past probability.

Der Hund wird wohl sieben Jahre alt gewesen sein.
The dog was probably seven years old.

Er wird wohl zufrieden gewesen sein.
He was probably satisfied.

PITFALL

The future, unlike English, is not used to make a request. Forms of *wollen* or *mögen* are used instead.

Wollen (möchten) Sie in meinen Garten kommen?
Will you come into my garden?

Wollen Sie jetzt bitte aufstehen?
Will you stand up now please?

PITFALL

German, unlike English and the Romance languages, never uses forms of "to go" to express the future. Use the future or the present with future implication.

Er wird es morgen tun.
He's going to do it tomorrow.

Er kommt morgen.
He's coming tomorrow   *or*   He's going to come tomorrow.

CONDITIONAL TENSE

RULE

English distinguishes between *should* (first person singular and plural) and *would* in the conditional. German does not use *sollen*. Conditional "would" or "should" in the first person singular and plural, are expressed by the following forms:

ich würde	wir würden
du würdest	ihr würdet
er würde	sie würden

These are the imperfect subjunctive, or subjunctive II forms of *werden*. *Werden* is thus the auxiliary for both the future and the conditional. In the following two examples, American English uses the forms *would* and *wouldn't* more frequently than the forms *should* and *shouldn't*.

Wir würden es gerne tun.
We would ("should") be glad to do it.

Das würde ich nicht sagen.
I wouldn't ("shouldn't") say that.

PITFALL

Nor is the German conditional used to render the English "should" when it indicates obligation. In such cases *sollen* is correct.

Sie sollten an die Arbeit gehen.
You should get to work.

Er sollte es so bald wie möglich tun.
He should do it as soon as possible.

PITFALL

Subjunctive II (imperfect subjunctive) can substitute for conditional *würde* constructions. These forms are preferred with the auxiliaries *haben* and *sein* (*hätte* and *wäre*) but not for most other verbs, since they are a little pompous, especially in conversation.

Ich würde ihm gerne helfen.
I would help him gladly.

Wir würden es lieber jetzt tun.
We would rather do it now.

These forms are preferable to *Ich hülfe ihm gerne* and *Wir täten es lieber jetzt.*

PITFALL

The imperfect (past) is used for repeated, habitual, or customary action in the past. One possible translation for the imperfect in English is "would," as in, "Jack Sprat would eat no fat/His wife would eat no lean." This is not a conditional "would," and must not be translated by *würde.*

Er sprach immer sehr leise zu mir, wenn er nach Hause kam.
He would always speak very gently to me when he came home.

> Sie brachte uns immer etwas mit, wenn sie uns besuchte.
> She would always bring us something when she visited us.

IMPERATIVE MOOD

> **RULE**
>
> Since there are three ways of saying "you" in German (see Personal Pronouns, p. 83) there are three ways of giving commands. An exclamation point is placed after commands.

> **Sag** (*Sage,* more formally) **die Antwort!** (familiar singular)
> **Sagt die Antwort!** (familiar plural)
> **Sagen Sie die Antwort!** (polite, singular and plural)

All three mean, "Say the answer."

The *ihr-* and *Sie-* imperatives are identical with their indicative forms. The *du-* imperative is, in most cases, the indicative form without -*st.* The imperative of *sein* is irregular; its forms are subjunctival.

> **Sei ruhig!**
> **Seid ruhig!**
> **Seien Sie ruhig!**

All three mean, "Be quiet."

> **RULE**
>
> If one includes one's self in a command, the *wir* form is used with the verb first.

> **Gehen wir jetzt nach Hause!**
> Let's go home now.
>
> **Machen wir zuerst die Arbeit fertig!**
> Let's finish the job first.

> **RULE**
>
> Do not use *tun* to translate English "don't" in negative commands.

Trinken Sie nicht so viel!
Don't drink so much.

Sagen Sie nichts davon!
Don't say anything about it.

RULE

The pronouns are usually omitted in the *du* and *ihr* imperatives. In the polite imperative, *Sie* is never omitted.

Spiel nicht mehr! (familiar singular)
Spielt nicht mehr! (familiar plural)
Spielen Sie nicht mehr! (polite, singular and plural)

RULE

Whenever *du* and *ihr* are used with the imperative to express emphasis, the order is the reverse of English.

Spiel du jetzt was auf dem Klavier!
Now you play something on the piano.

Geht ihr jetzt nach Hause; wir folgen euch bald!
You go home now; we'll follow you soon.

Note: In older religious writing in English where the "thou" form is used, the order is the same as in German.

Befiehl du deine Wege (Paul Gerhardt)
Commend thou thy ways

RULE

In colloquial speech the *du* imperative drops the *-e* but the form with or without *-e* is possible. Strong verbs which change their stem vowel from *e* to *i* or *ie* (see Present Tense, p. 103) also change the vowel in the *du* imperative but *never* have an *-e* ending.

Sprich lauter!	**Wirf mir den Ball!**	**Nimm den Ring!**
Speak louder.	Throw me the ball.	Take the ring.

Triff noch einmal! (v. Hofmannsthal's Electra to her brother Orestes)
Strike again.

This is also true of *sehen* "to see" but *siehe* instead of *sieh* is used in exclamations ("behold") and in giving references in books: *siehe Seite 36* — see page 36.

More imperious alternates for the imperative are the past participle and the infinitive. These are often peremptory and are used generally by persons in authority as commands to subordinates. They are less common today than formerly.

Aufstehen!		**Aufmachen!**	
Aufgestanden!	"Get up."	**Aufgemacht!**	"Open up."

The infinitive is also used as polite imperative in directions and recipes (*Kochrezepte*):

Kühl und trocken aufbewahren.
Store in a cool dry place.

An der Goethestraße links abbiegen.
Turn left at Goethestraße.

Eiskalt servieren.
Serve very cold.

VERBS WITH PREFIXES

There are three types of prefixes in German: **inseparable, separable,** and doubtful. The inseparable prefixes are: *be-, emp-, ent-, er-, ge-, miß, ver-,* and *zer-*. Never stress an inseparable prefix in pronunciation. The first syllable of the basic verb is stressed: *begínnen; empféhlen; entságen; erdíchten; gewínnen; mißráten; verstéhen; zerbröckeln.*

RULE

Inseparable prefix verbs never add a *ge-* in the past participle.

Er hat die Geschichte erfunden.
He invented the story.

Er hat uns belogen und betrogen.
He lied to us and deceived us.

Sie haben die Mädchen nicht aus dem Serail entführt.
They didn't abduct the girls from the seraglio (harem).

Der Richter hat den Krug zerbrochen.
The judge shattered the pitcher.

PITFALL

Verbs with the inseparable prefix *ge-* retain it in *all* their forms.
Do not confuse these verbs with the ones without the *ge-* prefix
which resemble them.

bieten (to offer, bid)	**gebieten** (to command)
brauchen (to need)	**gebrauchen** (to use)
fallen (to fall)	**gefallen** (to be pleasing, like)
horchen (to hearken)	**gehorchen** (to obey)
hören (to hear)	**gehören** (to belong)
raten (to advise)	**geraten** (to get into; turn out)
reichen (to reach)	**gereichen** (to redound to)
stehen (to stand)	**gestehen** (to confess)

Since the meaning of prefix verbs can vary widely, context usually will help to keep them straight.

Es hat dem Volk sehr gefallen, daß der Tyrann gefallen war.
The people were very glad that the tyrant had fallen.

PITFALL

The prefix *ver-* can cause several changes in meaning. These are
sometimes referred to as "wrong or strong."

Wrong

Der Präsident hat sich versprochen.
The President misspoke himself.

Er hat versungen und vertan. (Wagner, *Die Meistersinger*)
He goofed (failed) in his singing and his chance for the prize.

Strong

Der Präsident hat schnelle Hilfe versprochen.
The President promised speedy assistance.

Ver- is also used to denote change in a condition, as in *verlängern* (to lengthen), *verschönern* (to beautify), and *vergrößern* (to enlarge).

Separable Prefixes

Separable prefixes are words in their own right, usually prepositions or adverbs, such as *an, auf, aus, bei, mit, nach, weg, zu.*

To indicate a verb with a separable prefix, grammar books usually insert a hyphen between the prefix and the infinitive of the basic verb: *an-kommen, aus-ziehen, ein-brechen.* This is only a grammar book convention. Write them as one word: *ankommen, ausziehen, einbrechen.*

RULE

If the infinitive is used with *zu,* it is placed between the prefix and the infinitive of the main verb and written as one word.

Morgens ist es ihr schwer aufzustehen.
It's difficult for her to get up in the morning.

Abends ist es ihm schwer einzuschlafen.
It's difficult for him to fall asleep at night.

The past participle is also written as one word with the prefix first.

Sie ist spät aufgestanden.
She got up late.

Er ist früh eingeschlafen.
He fell asleep early.

RULE

English is often very free with respect to the position of a separable prefix. "He shuts off the water" and "He shuts the water off" mean the same thing. In German, however, there is no choice of wording.* In the present, past (imperfect), and imperative, the prefix is placed at the end of the sentence. In subordinate clauses, however, the entire verb form is last.

Zieh dir den Mantel an.
Put your coat on. (Put on your coat.)

*Some modern authors (Expressionist, etc.) often wrench word order to jolt their readers.

Sie schossen das Flugzeug ab.
They shot down the plane. (They shot the plane down.)

Er bringt immer seine Freunde mit.
He always brings his friends along. (He always brings along his
friends.)

Subordinate Clauses

**Ich weiß nicht, ob sie das Flugzeug abschossen. (abgeschossen
haben)**
I don't know if they shot down the plane.

Ich weiß, daß er immer seine Freunde mitbringt.
I know that he always brings his friends along.

Doubtful Prefixes

Durch-, hinter-, um-, unter-, über-, and *zwischen-* may be encountered as
separable or inseparable. They are therefore called "variable" or "doubtful." When they are used in a literal sense and when the stress is not on the
verb but on the prefix, they are separable. When they are used in a figurative sense and the stress remains on the verb, they are inseparable. Verbs
with variable prefixes thus have two meanings. Contrast the following:

Literal Meaning

Der Fährmann hat die Gäste übergesetzt.
The ferryman carried the guests across.

Er hat die Koffer wiedergeholt.
He fetched the suitcases again.

Wir schauten die Zeitungen durch.
We looked through the newspapers.

Figurative Meaning

Wir haben die Gedichte übersetzt.
We translated the poems.

Er hat den Satz wiederholt.
He repeated the sentence.

Wir durchschauten die Zeitungsenten.
We saw through the newspaper canards (hoaxes).

Fortunately, there are not too many doubtful prefix verbs. All good dictionaries indicate whether a doubtful prefix verb is separable, inseparable, or both.

THE SUBJUNCTIVE AND ITS TENSES

The indicative tenses state a fact or ask a question about it. The subjunctive is used for unreal or contrary-to-fact conditions, indirect discourse, and often when there is doubt or uncertainty in the mind of the speaker. Except for the verb "to be," the subjunctive is vestigial in English. "May," "might," and "would" are used in most subjunctive situations in English. Although some people are dedicated to preservation of the subjunctive, it is fading. It is still used in official and formal writing. In English it differs only slightly from the indicative by the absence of an -*s* in the third person singular, as the following examples show:

He was released on condition that he never return to New Jersey.

I demand that my subconscious mind negate and release all discordant patterns.

Careful speakers of English still use it in contrary-to-fact conditions, for example, "If I *were* you, I would see to it right away."

Although many subjunctive forms in German show signs of atrophy in the spoken language, in comparison to English, the subjunctive is alive and well.

There has been considerable variation in naming the subjunctive forms. The traditional names parallel the names of the tenses of the indicative mood. Most newer grammar texts, however, refer to Subjunctive I (or Primary) and Subjunctive II (or Secondary). In fact, Subjunctive II is much more frequently used than Subjunctive I. For that reason some texts call Subjunctive II the General Subjunctive and Subjunctive I the Special Subjunctive. The ending pattern for all verbs in the subjunctive is the same: -*e*, -*est*, -*e*; -*en*, -*et*, -*en*.

> **RULE**
>
> Only Subjunctive I can be used for the so-called hortatory or optative subjunctive.

It translates as "may" or "let" in English and is found in older literature and in certain phrases. *Sollen* with the infinitive is more commonly used in modern spoken German.

Er stehe fest und sehe hier sich um. (Goethe, *Faust II*)
Let him stand fast and look about him here.

Sie komme, sie töte mich! (Schiller, *Maria Stuart*)
Let her come! Let her kill me!

Es lebe der König (die Republik, die Liebe)!
Long live the king (the republic, love)!

RULE

German uses the subjunctive in indirect discourse while English does not. Either Subjunctive I or II may be used.

Direct discourse

Der Angeklagte sagte, „Ich war nie da."
The accused said: "I was never there."

Der Angeklagte sagte, „Ich habe es nicht getan."
The accused said: "I didn't do it."

Indirect discourse

Der Angeklagte sagt, er wäre (sei) nie da gewesen.
The accused said that he had never been there.

Der Angeklagte sagte, er habe (hätte) es nicht getan.
The accused said he didn't do it.

The rationale behind this is that if a statement is not a direct quote and if someone else is reporting the words of another, there is the possibility of error.

PITFALL

Forms of Subjunctive I of *sein* are irregular.

ich sei	wir seien
du seiest	ihr seiet
er sei	sie seien

PITFALL

Subjunctive II (imperfect subjunctive) forms of weak verbs are identical with the forms of the past indicative (imperfect).

Indicative

Sie zeigte mir den Brief.
She showed me the letter.

Er spielte mit den Kindern.
He played with the children.

Subjunctive

Wenn du mir den Brief zeigtest . . .
If you showed me the letter . . .

Wenn er mit den Kindern spielte . . .
If he played with the children . . .

Strong verbs add subjunctive endings to the past and add an umlaut if possible.

Indicative	Subjunctive
sprach	spräche
ging	ginge
tat	täte
trug	trüge

PITFALL

A few strong verbs have irregular Subjunctive II forms.

Infinitive	Past	Subjunctive II
beginnen	begann	begönne
gewinnen	gewann	gewönne
helfen	half	hülfe
schelten	schalt	schölte
schwimmen	schwamm	schwömme
schwören	schwor	schwüre
spinnen	spann	spönne
stehen	stand	stünde
sterben	starb	stürbe

verderben	verdarb	verdürbe
werben	warb	würbe
werfen	warf	würfe

Many of these irregular forms are obsolete. In conversation, *sollte*, *würde*, or *könnte* are often substituted.

Wenn ich das Spiel gewinnen sollte (instead of *gewönne*) . . .
If I won the game . . . *or* If I should win the game . . .

Wenn er jetzt vor mir stehen würde (instead of *stünde*) . . .
If he stood before me now . . . *or* If he were standing before me now . .

PITFALL
   Four of the modals add an umlaut in forming Subjunctive II (imperfect subjunctive). Two, *sollen,* and *wollen,* do not.

dürfte	möchte
könnte	müßte

But:

sollte
wollte

RULE
   Subjunctive II (imperfect subjunctive) can be used instead of the conditional.

These forms are considered polite, identical to English usage. Subjunctive II is more frequently used than the conditional with *kommen, wissen,* the six modals, and especially with *haben* and *sein* to express "would."

Subjunctive II

Könnten Sie mir Auskunft darüber geben?
Could you give me information about it?

Wüßten Sie die Antwort?
Would you know the answer?

Wäre das möglich?
Would that be possible?

Ich hätte ihn gerne gesehen.
I would have been glad to see him.

Conditional

Würden Sie mir Auskunft darüber geben können?
Could you give me information about it?

Würden Sie die Antwort wissen?
Would you know the answer?

Würde das möglich sein?
Would that be possible?

Ich würde ihn gerne gehesen haben.
I would have been glad to see him.

A frequent use of the subjunctive is in contrary-to-fact conditions (see Conditional, p. 112). In conditions that refer to present or future events, German uses the subjunctive in the "if" clause and *würde* + infinitive in the conclusion.

Wenn ich Zeit hätte, würde ich es tun.
If I had time I would do it.

Wenn er hier wäre, würden wir ihm helfen.
If he were here we would help him.

For past conditions *hätte* or *wäre* is used with the past participle.

Wenn ich Zeit gehabt hätte, würde ich es getan haben.
If I had had time I would have done it.

Wenn er hier gewesen wäre, würden wir ihm geholfen haben.
If he had been here we would have helped him.

MODAL AUXILIARIES

The word *modal* is the adjectival form of mood and the word *auxiliary* means helping verb. The modals thus express states of mind or moods, such as probability, possibility, desiring, wanting, etc.

Present Tense of the Modals

dürfen (to be permitted to, may)

ich darf   wir dürfen

du darfst   ihr dürft
er darf   sie dürfen

können (to be able, can)

ich kann	wir können
du kannst	ihr könnt
er kann	sie können

mögen (to like)

ich mag	wir mögen
du magst	ihr mögt
er mag	sie mögen

müssen (to have to, must)

ich muß	wir müssen
du mußt	ihr müßt
er muß	sie müssen

sollen (to be supposed to, should, ought)

ich soll	wir sollen
du sollst	ihr sollt
er soll	sie sollen

wollen (to want)

ich will	wir wollen
du willst	ihr wollt
er will	sie wollen

RULE

Four of these verbs—*dürfen, können, mögen,* and *müssen*—have umlauts in the infinitive but not in the past (imperfect) or in the three persons of the singular of the present tense. In the present, the first and third person singular do not have regular present tense endings in -*e* and -*t*. In this respect they resemble their English cognates in the third person singular, which also lack the ending -*s*.

er kann	er muß	er soll
he can	he must	he should

In the present tense, all but *sollen* change the vowel of the infinitive in the singular.

PITFALL

These verbs are "defective" in English, i.e., they do not have forms for all the tenses, whereas in German, forms exist in all the tenses. Since "must," "should," "ought," "can," and "could" are limited to certain tenses, you must translate many modal forms with other English equivalents or paraphrases. You will have no trouble with the following:

Darf ich Sie nach Hause begleiten?
May I see you home?

Sie kann ihn nicht leiden.
She can't stand him.

Ich konnte viel lernen.
I could study a lot.

Ich muß viel lernen.
I must study a lot.

Ich soll viel lernen.
I am supposed to study a lot.

But for the other tenses it is necessary to use forms of "to be permitted" for *dürfen,* "to be able" for *können,* and "to have to" for *müssen.* For *sollen,* equivalents such as "to be supposed to," "to be to," "to be expected to," are required.

Ich habe Sie nach Hause begleiten dürfen.
I was permitted to see you home.

Sie wird ihn nicht leiden können.
She won't be able to stand him.

Ich mußte viel lernen.
I had to study a lot.

Ich werde viel lernen müssen.
I will have to study a lot.

Ich habe viel lernen müssen.
I had to study a lot.

Ich hätte viel lernen sollen.
I should have studied a lot.

Ich werde viel lernen sollen.
I will be expected to study a lot.

RULE

The preposition *zu* (to) is never used in German before an infinitive dependent on a modal.

Er will jetzt gehen.
He wants to go now.

Sie darf nichts mitbringen.
She may not bring along anything.

Er möchte seine Tante besuchen.
He would like to visit his aunt.

Wir mußten das Gedicht auswendig lernen.
We had to memorize the poem.

PITFALL

The complementary infinitive after a modal auxiliary comes at the end of the sentence or clause, unless the modal is used in a subordinate clause in which case the finite or conjugated verb (the modal) comes at the end, after the infinitive.

Ich kann nichts mehr für ihn tun.
I can do no more for him.

Sie will ihr Lied singen.
She wants to sing her song.

But in subordinate clauses:

Ich war traurig, weil ich nichts mehr für ihn tun konnte.
I was sad because I couldn't do anything more for him.

Sie sagt, daß sie ihr Lied singen will.
She says that she wants to sing her song.

PITFALL

Do not confuse German modal forms *will* and *soll* with English "shall" and "will." German uses the present of *werden* to form the future. (See Future in this chapter, p. 110.)

Ich werde ihn sehen wollen.
I will want to see him.

Ich werde ihn sehen sollen.
I will be expected to see him.

PITFALL

Modals have two past participles, one in *ge...t* and another which is identical with the infinitive. The latter is used in so-called "double infinitive" constructions. When a complementary infinitive is present, the *ge...t* forms cannot be used.

Without complementary infinitive

Ich habe es nicht gewollt. (William II, German Emperor, referring to World War I)
I didn't want it.

Sie hat nicht die Kirschen, sondern die Äpfel gewollt.
She didn't want the cherries but the apples.

With complementary infinitive

Ich habe nicht kämpfen wollen.
I didn't want to fight.

Sie hat die Kirschen essen wollen.
She wanted to eat the cherries.

RULE

When the double infinitive construction is used in a subordinate clause, the finite verb immediately precedes the two infinitives.

Sie war böse, weil er ihr seinen Mantra nicht hat sagen wollen.
She was angry because he wouldn't tell her his mantra.

Es ist schade, daß wir nicht haben gehen können.
It's a pity that we couldn't go.

Sie schimpften, weil sie viel haben arbeiten müssen.
They complained because they had to work a lot.

This pile-up of verbs at the end of a sentence is usually avoided in a variety of ways. The simplest and most common way is to use the imperfect (past).

Sie war böse, weil er ihr seinen Mantra nicht sagen wollte.
She was angry because he wouldn't tell her his mantra.

Es ist schade, daß wir nicht gehen konnten.
It's a pity that we couldn't go.

Sie schimpften, weil sie viel arbeiten mußten.
They complained because they had to work a lot.

> RULE
>
> When there is a change of subject, German must use a *daß* clause with *wollen* and *mögen*.

Contrast the following:

Ich will es tun. (no change of subject)
I want to do it.

Ich will, daß Sie es tun. (change of subject)
I want you to do it.

PITFALL

Dürfen means "to be allowed." *Lassen* means "to allow."

Er darf jetzt gehen.
He may (is allowed to) go now.

Laß ihn gehen!
Let (allow) him go.

PITFALL

Müssen can translate as "must" except when negative. Then it is translated as "not to have to" (no obligation). To express prohibition (*must not*) use *dürfen*.

Du mußt es nicht tun.
You don't have to do it. (no obligation)

Du darfst es nicht tun.
You mustn't do it. (prohibition—you're not allowed to)

Du mußt nicht unbedingt dieses Hemd tragen.
You don't absolutely have to wear this shirt.

Du darfst dieses Hemd nicht tragen. Es gehört mir und ist ein Geschenk von Nessus und Medea.
You mustn't wear this shirt. It belongs to me and is a gift from Nessus and Medea.

RULE

English "could" is used in two senses. When "could" is a past tense and means "was able," use the German past tense *konnte.* When it means "would be able" or "might be able," use the subjunctive *könnte.*

Past tense (imperfect)

Er konnte es nicht tun.
He couldn't do it.

Ich konnte nicht dorthin kommen.
I couldn't get there.

Subjunctive

Er könnte es tun, wenn er wollte.
He could do it if he wanted to.

Ach könnte ich dorthin kommen . . . (Heine)
Oh could I but get there . . . (If I were only able to get there . . .)

Idiomatic Uses of Modals

RULE

Frequently modals are used by themselves with a verb like *gehen, fahren* or *tun* implied or understood.

Wir müssen jetzt fort.
We must go away now. (Compare old-fashioned English, "We must away.")

Sie kann heute nicht ins Theater.
She can't go to the theater today.

Wir wollen's und können's.
We want to do it and can.

Wollen is used in the meaning "to claim to."

Sie will eine Prinzessin sein.
She claims to be a princess.

Sie wollen ihn dort gesehen haben.
They claim to have seen him there.

Können is used idiomatically with languages in the meaning "to know." It also conveys the idea of "know-how," "ability," "skill."

Er kann Französisch.
He knows French.

Sie kann kein Griechisch.
She knows no Greek.

Können is often used idiomatically for *dürfen,* just as "can" is frequently used for "may" in English.

Können (Dürfen) wir jetzt gehen?
Can (May) we go now?

PASSIVE VOICE

A verb is said to be in the **passive voice** when the grammatical subject is acted upon, rather than doing the acting. As in English, only transitive verbs can be made passive.

Active

Hans sees Paul.
Hans sieht Paul.

Heinz loves Susanne.
Heinz liebt Susanne.

They built a house.
Sie bauten ein Haus.

Passive

Paul is seen by Hans.
Paul wird von Hans gesehen.

Susanne is loved by Heinz.
Susanne wird von Heinz geliebt.

A house was built by them.
Ein Haus wurde von ihnen gebaut.

RULE

English uses "to be" but German uses *werden* "to become" as the auxiliary in the passive.

Er wird von allen geliebt.
He is loved by all.

Er wurde von allen Frauen geliebt.
He was loved by all women.

PITFALL

Remember that *werden* is a *sein* verb and that perfect tenses of the passive use forms of *sein*, not *haben.*

Er ist von allen gelobt worden.
He was praised by all. *Or:* He has been praised by all.

Er war von allen gelobt worden.
He had been praised by all.

All German present perfect tenses, active or passive, may frequently be translated by an English past tense.

PITFALL

In the perfect tenses of the passive, the past participle of werden drops the *ge-.*

Das Haus ist gebaut worden.
The house has been built.

RULE

Ward can be used for *wurde* in poetry and older literatuare. It is used in the singular. The forms *wurden* and *wurdet* must be used in the plural.

**Belsazar ward aber in selbiger Nacht
Von seinen Knechten umgebracht.** (Heine)
But on that same night Belshazar
was done in by his henchmen.

RULE

The personal agent "by" in the passive is expressed by the preposition *von*. Do not use *bei*.

Er wurde von allen begrüßt.
He was greeted by all.
Das Buch wird von ihr geschrieben werden.
The book will be written by her.

RULE

If the agent in the passive is not a human or if the means or instrument by which an action is accomplished is emphasized, *durch* + accusative is used.

Er wurde durch eine Explosion getötet.
He was killed by an explosion.
Sie wurden durch Liebe geheilt.
They were cured by love.

RULE

German distinguishes between a "false" or "apparent" passive and a true passive. The former describes the result of an action and uses the past participle adjectivally with *sein*. The latter, the true passive, indicates an action, not a condition or state of being, and uses forms of *werden*. If you can insert "being," it is a true passive.

False Passive
Das Lokal ist geschlossen.
The bar is closed. (describes the state of the bar—not an action)

Das Geschäft war ausgebrannt und geplündert.
The store was burned out and plundered. (describes its state—how it was found)

True Passive

Das Lokal wird geschlossen.
The bar is (being) closed.

Das Geschäft wurde ausgebrannt und geplündert.
The business was (being) burned and plundered.

RULE

　Both *sein* and *werden* can be used with the past participle *geboren* (born). Use *sein* for living persons and *werden* for the dead.

Goethe wurde im Jahre 1749 geboren.
Goethe was born in the year 1749.

Schiller wurde im Jahre 1759 geboren.
Schiller was born in 1759.

Meine Verlobte ist im Jahre 1939 geboren.
My fiancée was born in 1939.

Wann bist du geboren?
When were you born?

Ich bin 1932 geboren.
I was born in 1932.

Colloquial German, like the Romance languages, makes less use of the passive than English. The impersonal pronoun *man* with an active verb is the most common substitution for the passive. (See Pronouns, p. 88.)

Hier spricht man Deutsch.
German is spoken here.

Man kann nichts daran ändern.
Nothing can be changed about it.

Other Substitutes for the Passive:

1. *verlorengehen* (to be lost)
   Der wahre Ring ist wahrscheinlich verlorengegangen.
   The genuine ring has probably been lost.

2. verbs used reflexively with an inanimate subject:
   Das erklärt sich nicht so leicht.
   That is not so easily explained.

3. *sich lassen* with an infinitive:
   Das läßt sich nicht so ohne weiteres machen.
   That can't be done quite so simply.

PITFALL

A German active infinitive with *zu* must sometimes be translated by a passive infinitive in English. Sometimes either an active or a passive infinitive can be used in English.

Das ist nicht zu glauben.
That is not to be believed. (*not* active infinitive "to believe")

Es war niemand zu sehen.
There was no one to be seen. (*not* active infinitive "to see")

Das ist leicht zu sagen.
That's easy to say. (the active infinitive is possible here)

Es gibt noch viel zu tun.
{There is still much to do. (either the active or passive
{There's still much to be done. infinitive is possible here)

Impersonal Verbs

German and English use many impersonal verb constructions.

Es regnet.   **Es schneit.**
It's raining.   It's snowing.

German, however, uses more of them than English, including many which cannot be translated literally, for example:

fehlen (to be lacking)   **gelingen** (to be successful)
gefallen (to be pleasing)   **gelten** (to be valid, applicable)

Es fehlt mir an Zeit und Geld.
I'm short of time and money.

Es gefällt uns zu Hause am besten.
We're happiest at home. (*literally:* It is most pleasing to us . . .)

Jetzt gilt es zu entscheiden.
Now the thing is to decide. (A decision must be made.)

Es gelang mir nicht, ihn zu finden.
I didn't succeed in finding him.

Sein and *gehen* are also used impersonally in idiomatic constructions:

Es ist (*or: geht*) ihm besser.
He's feeling better.

Verbs with a Dative Object

PITFALL

Some German verbs always take a dative object although the English would lead you to expect an accusative. The most common ones are the following:

antworten (to answer)	**glauben** (to believe)
befehlen (to order)	**gleichen** (to resemble)
begegnen (to meet)	**gratulieren** (to congratulate)
danken (to thank)	**helfen** (to help)
dienen (to serve)	**nützen** (to be of use; utilize)
drohen (to threaten)	**passen** (to fit)
fehlen (to be lacking)	**raten** (to advise)
folgen (to follow)	**schaden** (to harmful)
gefallen (to be pleasing)	**vertrauen** (to trust)
gehorchen (to obey)	**verzeihen** (to excuse)
gehören (to belong)	**wehtun** (to hurt)
gelingen (to succeed)	**widersprechen** (to contradict)

The rationale for the dative is that one gives help, thanks, orders, advice, congratulations, etc., to someone.

Helfen Sie ihm bei seiner Arbeit!
Help him with his work.

Wir danken Ihnen sehr.
We thank you very much.

Du gleichst dem Geist, den du begreifst. (Goethe, *Faust*)
You resemble (are like) the spirit which you understand.

Der Lehrer hat mir geraten, fleißiger zu lernen.
The teacher advised me to study harder.

Ich gratulierte ihr zum Geburtstag.
I congratulated her on her birthday.

Verbs with a Genitive Object

Certain verbs take the genitive. Many of them are legal terms, for example, the following, which all mean "to accuse someone of a crime": *anklagen, beschuldigen,* and *bezichtigen.*

Other verbs with the genitive are the following:

bedürfen (to require, need)	sich erinnern (to remember)
entbehren (to lack)	gedenken (to think of)
sich erbarmen (to have mercy on)	versichern (to assure)

The genitive is increasingly avoided in modern German (see Prepositions, p. 68). Most verbs with the genitive are considered literary or old-fashioned. For example, *Brauchen* and *fehlen* are much more common than *bedürfen* and *entbehren* for "to need" and "to lack." It is more usual to say *Denk an mich* than *Gedenke meiner* (Think of me) and *Erinnern Sie sich an mich* than *Erinnern Sie sich meiner* (Remember me).

Special Uses of Verbs

Haben, sein, and *werden* are very important verbs which can be used by themselves or as auxiliaries.

RULE

Haben translates as "to be" in many idioms.

Angst haben (to be afraid)	**Glück haben** (to be lucky)
Durst haben (to be thirsty)	**recht haben** (to be right)
Er hat unrecht.	
He is wrong.	

If one said *"Er ist nicht richtig,"* that would mean that there was something wrong with him, that he was not "right in the head."

RULE

Sein translates as "to have" when used as the auxiliary verb in the perfect tenses. (See *sein-* verbs, p. 108.)

Sie ist in Frankfurt angekommen.
She (has) arrived in Frankfurt.

Sie war in Frankfurt angekommen.
She had arrived in Frankfurt.

Sie wird in Frankfurt angekommen sein.
She will have arrived in Frankfurt.

RULE

German *werden* must frequently be translated as "to be" in English.

(See Passive, p. 131.)

Was will er werden?
What does he want to be?

Sie ist eine große Malerin geworden.
She has become a great painter.
But:

Sie will Malerin werden.
She wants to be a painter.

Was nicht ist kann noch werden.
What isn't may yet be.

The distinction between "to be" and "to become" is made in both German and English. But German is generally more aware of it, as a humorous couplet by Wilhelm Busch illustrates:

Vater werden ist nicht schwer.
Vater sein dagegen sehr.

A free translation is "to become a father isn't hard at all, but being one is quite another matter."

Forms of *sein* and *werden* are used extensively in philosophy and poetry:

Genug des Werdens, laß mich sein! (M. Wesendonck)
Enough of becoming, let me be!

Philosophers and system builders sometimes specialize in making elaborate philosophical distinctions not only between *sein* and *werden* but also between *das Seiende* and *das Werdende, das Gewordene* and *das Gewesene,* etc. Participles (present and past) are adjectives which, in turn, can be used as nouns. (See adjectival nouns in the chapter on Adjectives, p. 7.)

Werden is also used to render English idiomatic uses of "to go" and "to get" (in the sense of "to become"), for example, "to go crazy" (*verrückt werden*) and "to get sick, rich," etc. (*krank, reich werden*).

PITFALL

Do not confuse the three verbs "to know."

Kennen means to know a person, place, book, etc., in the sense of being familiar or acquainted with it. It is cognate with the archaic English verb "ken" (*Do you ken John Peel?*).

Sie kennt ihn gut.
She knows him well.

Ich kenne Griechenland noch nicht.
I don't know Greece yet.

Er kennt Schillers Dramen nicht.
He doesn't know Schiller's plays.

Wissen means to know a fact, compare *Wissenschaft* (science, knowledge).

Ich kenne ihn nicht, aber ich weiß, wo er wohnt.
I don't know him, but I know where he lives.

Wissen Sie die Antwort?
Do you know the answer?

Zwar weiß ich viel, doch möchte ich alles wissen. (Goethe)
I do indeed know a lot, but I'd like to know everything.

Können means to know a language, with a verb like *sprechen, lesen* or *schreiben* understood. It also indicates "know-how," "skill."

Arabisch kann sie noch nicht.
She doesn't know Arabic yet.

Können Sie tanzen?
Do you know how to dance?

RULE

"There is" can be expressed in German either by *es gibt* + accusative or by *es ist* (*sind* in the plural) with the nominative. *Es gibt* is used if the person or thing is stressed and not the place. *Es gibt* emphasizes existence as such and is both singular and plural.

Es gibt Menschen, die so was zum Spaß machen.
There are people who do things like that for fun.

Es gibt immer noch Standesunterschiede.
There are still class distinctions.

Es gibt keinen stichhaltigen Grund dafür.
There is no valid reason for that.

With *es ist* or *es sind* the emphasis is on the place.

Es ist jemand an der Tür.
There is someone at the door.

Es ist eine Katze auf dem heißen Blechdach.
There's a cat on the hot tin roof.

Often, but not always, *es gibt* refers to more permanent conditions:

Es gibt Wölfe im Walde.
There are wolves in the forest. (They are always there.)

Es sind Wölfe im Walde.
There are wolves in the forest. (They are not usually there.)

RULE

Sprechen can mean "to see" (often briefly and/or in an official capacity). It then takes a direct object.

Ich kann Sie jetzt sprechen.
I can see you now.

Sprechstunde means "office hour" of professionals. Of course, "to talk with someone" is *sprechen mit* + dative.

> PITFALL
>
> *Umbringen* and *umkommen* are not to "bring round" and "to come round" but "to kill, do in," and "to die, perish."
>
> **Wenn du so weitermachst, bringst du mich noch um.**
> If you keep on like that, you'll kill me yet.
>
> **Viele sind bei dem Unfall umgekommen.**
> Many perished in the accident.
>
> There are many more such possible confusions. (See Vocabulary: Words Frequently Confused, and Prepositions, pp. 197 and 67.)

Omission of -*e*

In the preceding discussion of verb forms it was pointed out that a final -*e* is usually omitted in conversation in the first person singular of the present and in the *du* imperative. One reason for the fading of Subjunctive I (called Present or Special Subjunctive in some texts) is the fact that older forms exist which retain this -*e* in the indicative. If you are familiar with the cantatas of Bach you will have noted the many *ihr* imperatives ending in -*et* instead of -*t*, for example, #46 *Schauet und sehet*, #172 *Erschallet, ihr Lieder*, and #214 *Tönet, ihr Pauken*. Luther's famous carol is *Ihr Kinderlein kommet*. The second and third persons singular of the present tense also often have an extra -*e*-, for example, #120 *Gott, man lobet dich in der Stille*, #166 *Wo gehest du hin*, and *Jesus bleibet meine Freude* (the famous *Jesu, Joy of Man's Desiring*). These indicative forms are archaic but are occasionally used for literary effect. In modern German the forms *du gehest* and *ihr gehet* are considered subjunctives. Even within the same work the verb form may appear with or without the extra -*e*-; for example, in Mozart's *Die Zauberflöte* Tamino asks, "*Lebt denn Pamina noch?*" and the chorus replies, "*Pamina lebet noch!*"

There is a widespread tendency to drop an -*e* in the combinations -*ele* and -*ere*. Historically, verbs (infinitives) which ended in -*elen* and -*eren* now end in -*eln* and -*ern* (*wandeln, wandern*).

This variable German -e is also to some extent a regional variable since in the South many words that end in -e are often pronounced without it, for example, *die Freud'*, *heut'*, *die Sonn'*, etc. By contrast, in the dialect of Berlin, -e's are used even when they are wrong, for example, *Berlin macht Musike*. The optional -e on the dative singular of some nouns is also more popular in the North. (See Regionalisms, p. 208.)

The important thing to remember is that if -e- or -e is written, pronounce it. If it isn't written, don't pronounce it.

PRINCIPAL PARTS OF SOME STRONG VERBS
ARRANGED ACCORDING TO PATTERN OF CHANGE

I	Infinitive	Past (Imperfect)	Past Participle	3rd Singular Present
	ei	i	i	ei
A	beißen—*to cut*	biß	gebissen	beißt
	gleichen—*to equal*	glich	geglichen	gleicht
	gleiten*—*to glide*	glitt	ist geglitten	gleitet
	greifen—*to seize*	griff	gegriffen	greift
	kneifen—*to pinch*	kniff	gekniffen	kneift
	leiden—*to suffer*	litt	gelitten	leidet
	pfeifen—*to whistle*	pfiff	gepfiffen	pfeift
	reißen—*to tear*	riß	gerissen	reißt
	schleichen—*to sneak*	schlich	ist geschlichen	schleicht
	schleifen—*to polish*	schliff	geschliffen	schleift
	schmeißen—*to fling*	schmiß	geschmissen	schmeißt
	schneiden—*to cut*	schnitt	geschnitten	schneidet
	schreiten—*to stride*	schritt	ist geschritten	schreitet
	streichen—*to stroke*	strich	gestrichen	streicht
	streiten—*to quarrel*	stritt	gestritten	streitet
	weichen—*to yield*	wich	ist gewichen	weicht

* THE WEAK FORMS: gleiten, gleitete, ist gegleitet, gleitet, are now rarely found

B	bleiben—*to remain*	blieb	ist geblieben	bleibt
	gedeihen—*to thrive*	gedieh	ist gediehen	gedeiht
	leihen—*to lend*	lieh	geliehen	leiht
	meiden—*to avoid*	mied	gemieden	meidet

preisen—*to praise*	pries	gepriesen	preist
reiben—*to rub*	rieb	gerieben	reibt
scheiden—*to separate*	schied	geschieden	scheidet
scheinen—*to shine,* *seem*	schien	geschienen	scheint
schreiben—*to write*	schrieb	geschrieben	schreibt
schreien—*to scream*	schrie	geschrieen	schreit
schweigen—*to be silent*	schwieg	geschwiegen	schweigt
speien—*to spew*	spie	gespieen	speit
steigen—*to climb*	stieg	ist gestiegen	steigt
treiben—*to drive*	trieb	getrieben	treibt
weisen—*to point out*	wies	gewiesen	weist

II Infinitive	Past (Imperfect)	Past Participle	3rd Singular Present
ie	o*	o*	ie
biegen—*to bend*	bog	gebogen	biegt
bieten—*to offer*	bot	geboten	bietet
fliegen—*to fly*	flog	ist geflogen	fliegt
fliehen—*to flee*	floh	ist geflohen	flieht
fließen—*to flow*	floß	ist geflossen	fließt
frieren—*to freeze*	fror	gefroren	friert
genießen—*to enjoy*	genoß	genossen	genießt
gießen—*to pour*	goß	gegossen	gießt
kriechen—*to creep*	kroch	ist gekrochen	kriecht
riechen—*to smell*	roch	gerochen	riecht
schieben—*to push*	schob	geschoben	schiebt
schießen—*to shoot*	schoß	geschossen	schießt
schließen—*to close*	schloß	geschlossen	schließt
wiegen—*to weigh*	wog	gewogen	wiegt
ziehen—*to pull*	zog	gezogen	zieht

(Note change to g from h of infinitive in Past Tense and Past Participle)

* When one consonant follows *o* in the Past Tense and in the Past Participle, the *o* is a long *o*. When two consonants follow (ß is a double consonant), the *o* is short.

Other verbs which follow this pattern but do not have "ie" in the infinitive are:

saugen—*to suck*	sog	gesogen	saugt
saufen—*to drink*	soff	gesoffen	säuft
heben—*to lift*	hob	gehoben	hebt

EXCEPTION

liegen—*to lie*	lag	gelegen	liegt

III	Infinitive	Past (Imperfect)	Past Participle	3rd Singular Present
	i	**a**	**u**	**i**
A	binden—*to bind*	band	gebunden	bindet
	dringen—*to urge*	drang	ist gedrungen	dringt
	finden—*to find*	fand	gefunden	findet
	gelingen—*to succeed*	gelang	ist gelungen	gelingt
	klingen—*to ring*	klang	geklungen	klingt
	ringen—*to struggle*	rang	gerungen	ringt
	schwingen—*to swing*	schwang	geschwungen	schwingt
	singen—*to sing*	sang	gesungen	singt
	springen—*to jump*	sprang	ist gesprungen	springt
	stinken—*to stink*	stank	gestunken	stinkt
	trinken—*to drink*	trank	getrunken	trinkt
	zwingen—*to force*	zwang	gezwungen	zwingt
	i	**a**	**o**	**i**
B	beginnen—*to begin*	begann	begonnen	beginnt
	gewinnen—*to win*	gewann	gewonnen	gewinnt
	rinnen—*to run*	rann	ist geronnen	rinnt
	schwimmen—*to swim*	schwamm	ist geschwommen	schwimmt
	sinnen—*to meditate*	sann	gesonnen	sinnt
	spinnen—*to spin*	spann	gesponnen	spinnt

IV	Infinitive	Past (Imperfect)	Past Participle	3rd Singular Present
	e	**a**	**e**	**i, ie, e**
A	essen—*to eat*	aß	gegessen	ißt
	geben—*to give*	gab	gegeben	gibt

genesen—*to recover*	genas	ist genesen	genest
geschehen—*to happen*	geschah	ist geschehen	geschieht
lesen—*to read*	las	gelesen	liest
messen—*to measure*	maß	gemessen	mißt
sehen—*to see*	sah	gesehen	sieht
treten—*to step*	trat	ist getreten	tritt
vergessen—*to forget*	vergaß	vergessen	vergißt

	e	a	o	i, ie
B	befehlen—*to order*	befahl	befohlen	befiehlt
	bergen—*to save*	barg	geborgen	birgt
	brechen—*to break*	brach	gebrochen	bricht
	empfehlen—*to rec-ommend*	empfahl	empfohlen	empfiehlt
	helfen—*to help*	half	geholfen	hilft
	nehmen—*to take*	nahm	genommen	nimmt
	sprechen—*to speak*	sprach	gesprochen	spricht
	stehlen—*to steal*	stahl	gestohlen	stiehlt
	sterben—*to die*	starb	ist gestorben	stirbt
	treffen—*to meet, hit*	traf	getroffen	trifft
	verderben—*to spoil*	verdarb	verdorben	verdirbt
	werben—*to solicit*	warb	geworben	wirbt
	werfen—*to throw*	warf	geworfen	wirft

	Infinitive	Past (Imperfect)	Past Participle	3rd Singular Present
V		a	u	a	ä, a
	backen—*to bake*	buk	gebacken	bäckt
	fahren—*to travel*	fuhr	ist gefahren	fährt
	graben—*to dig*	grub	gegraben	gräbt
	schaffen—*to create*	schuf	geschaffen	schafft
	schlagen—*to beat*	schlug	geschlagen	schlägt
	tragen—*to carry*	trug	getragen	trägt
	wachsen—*to grow*	wuchs	ist gewachsen	wächst
	waschen—*to wash*	wusch	gewaschen	wäscht

	Infinitive	Past (Imperfect)	Past Participle	3rd Singular Present
VI		a	ie	a	ä
	blasen—*to blow*	blies	geblasen	bläst

braten—*to roast*	briet	gebraten	brät
fallen—*to fall*	fiel	ist gefallen	fällt
halten—*to hold*	hielt	gehalten	hält
lassen—*to let*	ließ	gelassen	läßt
raten—*to advise*	riet	geraten	rät
schlafen—*to sleep*	schlief	geschlafen	schläft

The following verbs, because they have the same change in the Past, and show the same vowel in the infinitive and past participle, are also listed in Group VI:

heißen—*to be called*	hieß	geheißen	heißt
laufen—*to run*	lief	ist gelaufen	läuft
rufen—*to call*	rief	gerufen	ruft
stoßen—*to push*	stieß	gestoßen	stößt

IRREGULAR VERBS WHICH DO NOT FIT INTO THE OTHER PATTERNS

VII Infinitive	Past (Imperfect)	Past Participle	3rd Singular Present
gehen—*to go*	ging	ist gegangen	geht
haben—*to have*	hatte	gehabt	hat
kommen—*to come*	kam	ist gekommen	kommt
sein—*to be*	war	ist gewesen	ist
tun—*to do*	tat	getan	tut
werden—*to become*	wurde	ist geworden	wird

PRINCIPAL PARTS OF MODAL AUXILIARIES

dürfen—*to be permitted*	durfte	gedurft, dürfen*	darf
können—*to be able*	konnte	gekonnt, können*	kann
mögen—*to like*	mochte	gemocht, mögen*	mag
müssen—*to have to*	mußte	gemußt, müssen*	muß
sollen—*to be supposed to*	sollte	gesollt, sollen*	soll
wollen—*to want*	wollte	gewollt, wollen*	will

* When immediately preceded by an infinitive.

SENTENCE STRUCTURE

8 ■ Word Order and Sentence Structure

WORD ORDER

Three types of word order—normal, inverted, and transposed—are distinguished in German.

RULE

Normal or Subject-Verb word order is used:
1. when the sentence begins with the subject (however short or long the subject may be)
2. after the coordinating conjunctions *und, aber, sondern, oder, denn*

Inverted or Verb-Subject word order is used:
1. in direct questions
2. whenever a word or phrase that is *not* the subject begins the sentence

In both normal and inverted word order, the verb is the *second* unit or element of the sentence.

PITFALL

Although the verb is the second unit of a declarative sentence (normal and inverted word order), the verb is not necessarily the second word.

Rudi trinkt viel Bier.
Rudi drinks a lot of beer.

Rudi und seine Kumpane im Studentenheim trinken viel Bier.
Rudi and his buddies in the dorm drink a lot of beer.

Die Frau sitzt auf der Bank.
The lady is sitting on the bench.

Die Frau im schönen, grünen Kleid mit den blauen Schleifen
sitzt auf der Bank.

The lady in the pretty green dress with the blue bows is sitting
on the bench.

RULE

In compound tenses the auxiliary verb is the second unit but infinitives and participles are placed at the end.

(See "Verbs," p. 106.)

Ich werde morgen den Brief schreiben.
I'll write the letter tomorrow.

Er hat zu viel Bier getrunken.
He drank too much beer.

Er will noch mehr trinken.
He wants to drink even more.

RULE

In subordinate clauses (transposed word order) the finite verb is placed at the end.

Er ist heute ruhig, weil er gestern zu viel Bier getrunken hat.
He's quiet today because he drank too much beer yesterday.

Ich weiß, daß er heute abend wieder trinken wird.
I know that he'll drink again tonight.

RULE

In subordinate clauses the conjugated or finite (inflected) verb occurs last. In the double infinitive construction, however, it precedes the two infinitives.

Wir waren empört, weil wir nichts haben sagen dürfen.
We were furious because we weren't allowed to say anything.

Er sagte, daß er die Arbeit nicht hat machen können.
He said that he couldn't do the work.

It is best to avoid this construction. (See Verbs: Modals, p. 129.)

PITFALL

English sentences usually start with the subject. In German, a sentence can start with the subject, a direct or indirect object, a prepositional phrase, adverbs, etc., depending on which element in the sentence is stressed. To avoid awkwardness when translating into English it is normally best to start with the subject, followed by the complete verb.

Die besten Sänger hat Toscanini selten gewählt.
Toscanini rarely chose the best singers.

Den ganzen Tag hab ich im Garten gearbeitet.
Im Garten hab ich den ganzen Tag gearbeitet.
I worked all day in the garden.

PITFALL

In literary, archaic, and religious writing in English where a sentence starts with an element other than the subject, the verb may or may not be the second unit or element. In German it always is the second unit.

Glad tidings bring I (I bring) unto you.
Frohe Botschaft bring ich euch.

Completely abolished from my consciousness is any feeling of inadequacy.
Ganz ausgeschlossen aus meinem Bewußtsein ist jegliches Gefühl der Unzulänglichkeit.

With wroth strode he through the throng.
Mit Zorn schritt er durch die Menge.

Aus der Fülle des Lebens wurde ich geboren und in der Fülle
des Lebens lebe ich wirksam und glücklich.
Out of the fullness of life was I born and in the fullness of life I live
effectively and happily.

In the last example the verb is the second unit of the English sentence (as it is in German), in the first clause after the prepositional
phrase. In the second clause the subject "I" is placed before the
verb. German must be consistent and uses inverted order in both
clauses.

PITFALL

Because German sentences begin with an element other than
the subject much more frequently than do English sentences, it is
essential to pay close attention to case forms, agreement between
verb and subject, and context, in order to identify the subject. (See
Articles, p. 21).

Die Kirschen haben die Kinder alle aufgegessen.
The children ate up all the cherries.

Zu viel Schnaps trinkt er.
He drinks too much alcohol.

Das Beste davon wird er sich aussuchen.
He'll pick out the best of it for himself.

Den Letzten beißen die Hunde.
The dogs will bite the last one. (Last one in is a rotten egg.)

Die bräutliche Schwester befreite der Bruder. (Wagner, *Die
Walküre*)
The brother has set free his sister and bride.

Contrast

Diese Werke machten Mendelssohn bekannt.
These works made Mendelssohn known.

Diese Werke machte Mendelssohn bekannt.
Mendelssohn made these works known.

In the first sentence *Werke* is the subject and Mendelssohn the
object, and the works in question would be Mendelssohn's own.

In the second example *Werke* is the object and would refer to Mendelssohn's programming of half-forgotten works of Bach and others. If the subject were singular, however, only the context would indicate the subject.

Dieses Werk machte Mendelssohn bekannt.
This work made Mendelssohn known. *Or:* Mendelssohn made this work known.

RULE

Transposed word order is used in all subordinate (dependent) clauses. In such cases the finite (conjugated or inflected) verb comes last. (See "Verbs," p. 106, and "Conjunctions," p. 38.) A subordinate clause may be introduced by:

    1. a subordinating conjunction (See "Conjunctions," p. 38.)
    2. a relative pronoun (See "Pronouns," p. 91.)
    3. an interrogative (question word) when it introduces an indirect question.

Direct and Indirect Questions

RULE

When interrogatives begin the sentence as a direct question, the verb comes second, as in English. When they pose indirect questions and introduce a clause, the finite verb comes at the end.

Direct Questions

„Wann geht der nächste Schwan?"
"When does the next swan leave?"

„Wo ist der Mann?"
"Where is the man?"

„Wie fährt man am besten?"
"What's the best way to get there?"

„Warum liebst du mich nicht mehr?"
"Why don't you love me any more?"

„Wem hat er das gesagt?"
"To whom did he say that?"

„Wer hat meine Uhr gestohlen?"
"Who stole my watch?"

„Was für Eier willst du haben?"
"How do you want your eggs?"

„Wie wurde der Westen gewonnen?"
"How was the West won?"

Indirect Questions

Leo Slezak, als Lohengrin, fragte, wann der nächste Schwan ging.
Leo Slezak, as Lohengrin, asked when the next swan was leaving.

Marlene Dietrich wollte wissen, wo der Mann ist.
Marlene Dietrich wanted to know where the man is.

Können Sie mir sagen, wie man am besten fährt?
Can you tell me the best way to get there?

Er fragte sie, warum sie ihn nicht mehr liebte.
He asked her why she didn't love him any more.

Gestehen Sie mir sofort, wem er das gesagt hat!
Tell me immediately to whom he said that.

Ich möchte feststellen, wer meine Uhr gestohlen hat.
I'd like to ascertain who stole my watch.

Er fragte Erda, was für Eier sie haben wollte.
He asked Erda what kind of eggs she wanted.

Es interessiert uns nicht, wie der Westen gewonnen wurde.
We're not interested in how the West was won.

RULE

When a sentence begins with a subordinate clause, the verb in the main clause comes first.

Another way of looking at it is to say that the subordinate clause is considered the first unit of the sentence and that the verb is the second unit.

Weil ich sie nicht sehen wollte, ging ich fort.
Because I didn't want to see them, I left.

Daß er im Grunde ein guter Mensch ist, weiß ich.
I know that he's basically a good person.

Während du im Hause arbeitest, gehe ich spazieren.
While you're working in the house, I'll go walking.

Wem er das gegeben hat, habe ich nicht erfahren können.
I couldn't ascertain to whom he gave it.

RULE

If the conjunction *wenn* (if) is omitted, the verb is placed at the beginning of the sentence.

The second clause often contains *so* or *dann.*

Willst das Zimmer mit mir teilen, Pudel laß das Heulen!
(Goethe)
If you want to share the room with me, poodle stop howling.

Kommt er heute, so erzähl ich ihm alles.
If he comes today I'll tell him everything.

Willst du nicht mein Bruder sein, so schlag' ich dir den Schädel ein.
If you won't be my brother I'll bash your head in.

PITFALL

When *daß*, or *ob* in the phrase *als ob* (as if) are omitted, transposed word order is not used, but the clause is still set off by commas, as are all subordinate clauses.

Ich weiß, er ist ein guter Mensch.
I know he's a good human being.

Sie sahen aus, als wären sie besoffen.
They looked as if they were drunk.

> **RULE**
>
> Unlike English, German adverbs may not intervene between subject and verb, and infinitives may not be split.

(See Adverbs, p. 16.)

Bellende Hunde beißen nicht.
Barking dogs don't bite.

Abends bleiben wir gewöhnlich zu Hause.
Evenings we usually stay at home.

authentisch zu schildern
to authentically depict

> **RULE**
>
> When both nouns are expressed in German, the indirect object (dative) always precedes the direct (accusative).

English can use two constructions, one with "to." It is wrong to use *zu* in German in the following examples:

Sie zeigt ihrer Mutter das Kleid.
She shows her mother the dress. *Or:* She shows the dress to her mother.

Faust und Mephisto schenken Gretchen den Schmuck.
Faust and Mephisto give Gretchen the jewelry. *Or:* Faust and Mephisto give the jewelry to Gretchen.

Er zeigte ihr seine Kupferstiche.
He showed her his etchings. *Or:* He showed his etchings to her.

Er gibt ihr einen Kuß und einen Nerzmantel.
He gives her a kiss and a mink. *Or:* He gives a kiss and a mink to her.

> **RULE**
>
> Infinitive phrases in English come first; however, in German they come last.

Wir hoffen, heute abend ins Theater gehen zu können.
We hope to be able to go to the theater tonight.

Es wäre besser, die Arbeit sofort zu tun.
It would be better to do the work right away.

Er weigerte sich, auf die Frage zu antworten.
He refused to answer the question.

Extended Adjective Construction

One of the most troublesome points of German usage is the **extended adjective construction** (also called extended attribute or participial construction). Germans could be faulted for gigantism linguistically on account of their huge compound nouns. Some German scholars are also given to the run-on sentence. Although most manuals of German style say that *Schachtelsätze* or convoluted sentences should be avoided, some, especially scholars, still favor them. Scholarly language in both East and West Germany still makes extensive use of the extended adjective construction, as witness a recent advertisement for a German periodical:

> **Die Zeitschrift veröffentlicht wissenschaftliche Originalarbeiten aus allen an der Universität vertretenen Fachdisziplinen.**
>
> *The periodical publishes original scientific papers from every university department.*

In language, the extended adjective construction still flourishes. Many editors and writers warn against the excessive use of adjectives because they feel that adjectives impede "getting on with the business" and retard the narrative flow. The flow can be even more retarded in German by overuse of the extended adjective construction.

It is often difficult to begin a novel in English since it may take a while to adjust to the author's style. Starting a novel in German can be even more difficult. Theodor Fontane's *Frau Jenny Treibel* is a case in point. About two-thirds of the novel consists of direct speech of the characters and is easier to read than the opening. On the very first page the reader finds two sentences with extended adjective constructions:

„An einem der letzten Maitage, das Wetter war schon sommer-
lich, bog ein zurückgeschlagener Landauer vom Spittel-
markt her in die Kur- und dann in die Adlerstraße ein und
hielt gleich danach vor *einem*, trotz seiner Front von nur
fünf Fenstern, ziemlich ansehnlichen, im übrigen aber
altmodischen *Hause*, dem ein neuer gelbbrauner Ölfar-
benanstrich wohl etwas mehr Sauberkeit, aber keine Spur
von gesteigerter Schönheit gegeben hatte, beinahe das
Gegenteil. "

„*Die* links sitzende *Dame* von etwa Dreißig, augenscheinlich
eine Erzieherin oder Gesellschafterin, öffnete von ihrem
Platz aus, zunächst den Wagenschlag und war dann *der*
anderen, mit Geschmack und Sorglichkeit gekleideten und
trotz ihrer hohen Fünfzig noch sehr gut aussehenden *Dame*
beim Aussteigen behilflich. "

In the first of these sentences you may have worked your way through to
einem (line 4). The problem is then to connect it with a noun, to answer the
question "stopped before a what?" The next nouns are *Front* and *Fenstern*.
It will help if you know that *Front* is feminine and that if the carriage had
stopped before a "front" the ending on *ein* would be *-er*, not *-em*. Since
Fenstern can only be dative plural (see "Nouns," p. 56) you can rule it out.
But the best way to connect *einem* with its noun is to identify the prepositional phrases: *trotz seiner Front* and *von nur fünf Fenstern*; this will lead you
to *Hause*.

In the second sentence the first extended adjective construction is not
difficult. *Die links sitzende Dame* cannot be translated literally as, "The on
the left sitting lady," but even if you did, you would be able to work it out
and rewrite it as, "The lady sitting on the left." The next extended adjective construction concerns the other lady (*der anderen . . . Dame*). Once
again, if you identify and separate the prepositional phrases you will understand the basic idea that the lady on the left was helpful to the other lady,
since the nouns *Geschmack*, *Sorglichkeit* and *Fünfzig* belong to the prepositional phrases *mit Geschmack und Sorglichkeit* and *trotz ihrer hohen Fünfzig*.

The ensemble of words dependent on a preposition is called a *prepositional phrase*. They are independent kingdoms exempt from other syntactic
considerations. Learning to recognize the boundaries of these kingdoms
will help you to decipher the long sentences for which German is famous.

This is particularly important when dealing with the extended adjective construction. Few speakers of English would say "for I" or "with I." Yet one does hear mistakes in English such as "with my friend and I," or "from my wife and I" because people fail to recognize prepositional phrases. Mark Twain is right when he says in *The Awful German Language* that "Prepositions are invested with an awful and unsuspected power." Twain cites an example from the German Queen of Kitsch, a 19th-century author, E. Marlitt. The extended adjective construction he quotes from her novel, *The Old Mamselle's Secret*, is not a complete sentence and contains several prepositional phrases:

> **„Wenn er aber auf der Straße der in Samt und Seide gehüllten jetzt sehr ungenirt nach der neusten Mode gekleideten Regierungsräthin begegnet . . ."**

Twain then translates it, adding hyphens and parentheses for the reader's assistance and amusement:

> *"But when he, upon the street, the (in-satin-and-silk-covered-now-very unconstrainedly-after-the-newest-fashion-dressed) government counselor's wife met . . ."*

If you can separate the prepositional phrases and the adverbs you can even get through thickets like that unscathed. Stick to the high ground of subject-verb-object and don't get bogged down. The basic idea is "he met the government counselor's wife." The prepositional phrase *auf der Straße* (on the street) tells where he met her. The other nouns *Samt, Seide,* and *Mode* belong to prepositional phrases with *in and nach* which describe how the lady is dressed. The article *der* is feminine dative and limits *Regierungsrätin. Begegnen* is a dative verb. (See "Verbs," p. 136.)

Extended adjective constructions usually contain a present or past participle used as an adjective. Often these participles are expanded by modifiers of their own, such as adverbs and prepositional phrases. Remember that if a participle is used as an adjective it is treated like any other adjective and may have either weak or strong endings. (See Adjectives, p. 2.) When translating extended adjective constructions into English, place the adjective after the noun, either directly or as a relative clause.

Alle hier angezeigten Bücher liefert jede Buchhandlung.
All books listed here any bookstore will deliver. *Or:* Any bookstore will deliver all books which are listed here.

der vom Richter zerbrochene Krug . . .
the pitcher broken by the judge . . . *Or:* the pitcher which was broken
    by the judge . . .

Extended adjective constructions are not unknown in English. Sometimes they occur as slightly playful complimentary closes in letters, for
example, "Your till all the wells run dry ever faithful friend." In one of the
many Viennese Graf Bobby jokes the count is asked to sign a financial
document. When he asks how to go about it, he is told to do just as he does
when signing a letter. He then promptly signs himself *Dein Dich liebender
Graf Bobby* (Your you loving Count Bobby). You may have seen constructions such as "The late but by all still lamented and lovingly remembered
friend and benefactor of this institution. . . ." A reference work speaks of
Schubert's "ahead of his time chord progressions." Legal language, of
course, uses phrases such as "the within named defendant," and "the there-
after to be designated parties." These are not effective in English, since,
when not meant to be humorous, they are pompous. If you attempt such
dazzling feats in German, you are likely to "pitfall." The extended adjective construction is rarely used in spoken German but is often found in
reference works and formal writing.

9 ■ Punctuation and Division into Syllables

English	Sign	German
period	.	der Punkt
question mark	?	das Fragezeichen
exclamation point	!	das Ausrufezeichen
comma	,	das Komma *or* der Beistrich
semicolon	;	das Semikolon *or* der Strichpunkt
colon	:	das Kolon *or* der Doppelpunkt
apostrophe	'	der Apostroph *or* der Auslassungszeichen
brackets	[ ]	eckige klammern
parentheses	( )	die Klammern
dash	—	der Gedankenstrich
suspension points	. . .	*die Auslassungspunkte
quotation marks	„ "	die Anführungszeichen (colloquially called *Gänsefüßchen* (little goose feet))

Punctuation marks are basically similar in English and German. There are, however, some differences and variations in their use. A few of the more common ones are noted here.

---

* English uses four suspension points or periods at the end of a sentence. German always uses only three.

159

RULE

In numerical expressions German uses a comma where English uses a period.

German	English
DM 8 *or* 8,-DM	8.00 German Marks
3,2%	3.2%

RULE

A comma marking off thousands and millions in English is replaced by a space in German.

German	English
4 790 824	4,790,824

PITFALL

Abbreviations are usually followed by a period. However, weights, measures, monetary units, points of the compass, chemical elements, and abbreviations spoken together as if they had formed a new word, have no punctuation mark after them.
BDR and *DDR* (*Bundesrepublik Deutschland* and *Deutsche Demokratische Republik*) are spoken like words, and no period is placed after them.

500 g	fünfhundert Gramm	(weight)
30 m	dreißig Meter	(measure)
DM 5,75	(monetary unit)	
Na	Natrium	(chemical element)
NNW	Nordnordwest	(point of the compass)

RULE

As in English, the comma is used to separate parts in a series. But unlike English, no comma is placed before *und* in such a series.

Frieda, Anna, Maria und Hilde sitzen schon im Zug.
Frieda, Anna, Maria, and Hilde are already sitting in the train.

RULE

All subordinate clauses, whether introduced by a subordinating conjuction, an interrogative, or a relative pronoun, are set off by commas (see Word Order, p. 147).

When *daß* and *ob* are omitted, the clause is still set off by commas, even though the finite verb is second.

Ich glaube, es ist zu früh.
I think it's too early.

Er tut, als wäre er besoffen.
He acts as if he were drunk.

RULE

The comma is used to set off modified participles and infinitives. If the participle is unmodified and if no words precede the infinitive, commas are not used.

Unmodified or alone

Entzückt schaute er sie an.
Fascinated, he looked at her.

Das Kind verließ weinend das Zimmer.
The child left the room weeping.

Sie beabsichtigt einzukaufen.
She plans to go shopping.

Modified

Von ihrer Schönheit entzückt, schaute er sie an.
The child left the room weeping loudly.

Das Kind verließ, laut weinend, das Zimmer.
The child left the room weeping loudly.

RULE

All infinitive phrases introduced by *um, ohne,* and *(an) statt* are set off by commas.

Wir arbeiten, um Geld zu verdienen.
We work to earn money.

Sie sagte, sie konnte nicht leben, ohne zu lieben.
She said she couldn't live without loving.

Die Ameise tanzte, statt zu arbeiten.
The ant danced instead of working.

RULE

In German, a dash is used in dialogues to denote a change of speakers.

—Ich will den ganzen Tag hier bleiben.
—Das ist leider nicht möglich.
—Na, dann eben ein andermal.

RULE

Unlike English, a colon, not a comma, precedes a direct quotation.

Sie sagte: „Ich will jetzt nicht."
She said, "I don't want to now."

Er fragte: „Warum nicht?"
He asked, "Why not?"

Als Bismarck den Titel Herzog von Lauenburg erhielt, sagte er:
„Diesen Titel werde ich benutzen, wenn ich inkognito reise."
When Bismarck received the title Duke of Lauenburg, he said, "I'll
use this title when I travel incognito."

Open quotes are written below the line; close quotes above the line.

Capitalization

RULE

In English, only proper nouns are capitalized. In German, all
nouns are capitalized.

This feature of German helps you to avoid confusing nouns with other
parts of speech. This is especially valuable for complex sentences or those
with extended adjective constructions.

PITFALL

All nouns are capitalized when they are used as nouns. When
used adverbially or adjectivally, they are not capitalized. Distinguish between the following:

Nouns	Adverbs
der Morgen	morgens
zu Mittag	mittags
am Donnerstag	donnerstags
spät am Abend	abends spät or spätabends
an einem Dienstagabend	Dienstag abends

When a language is used as a noun, it is capitalized. When it is
used as an adverb or adjective, it is not.

Noun	Adjective or Adverb
Er kann Deutsch.	Er hat es auf deutsch gesagt.

Wir verstehen schlecht Spanisch.	**Die spanische Sprache ist schön.**
Sie spricht Englisch.	**Das Buch ist englisch geschrieben.**

In many set phrases, adjectival nouns are not capitalized.

auf dem laufenden bleiben
to keep abreast of things

Alles bleibt beim alten.
Everything will remain as it was.

Sie fragte den ersten besten.
She asked the first person who came along.

den kürzeren ziehen to get the worst of it	**im großen und ganzen** on the whole
bei weitem by far	**im stillen** privately, on the quiet
im allgemeinen in general	**im trüben fischen** to fish in troubled waters

Note: There is an increasing tendency to capitalize any noun which can be preceded by an article or a *der-* or *ein-* word. Many linguists advocate this.

RULE

The polite form of address, *Sie,* is capitalized in all its cases and forms no matter where it occurs in a sentence.

Wenn ich Sie morgen sehe, gebe ich Ihnen Ihr Geld zurück.
If I see you tomorrow, I'll give you your money back.

Ich is not capitalized unless it begins a sentence or line of poetry.

RULE

Adjectives derived from names of countries are not capitalized.

Wollen Sie russischen oder persischen Kaviar?
Do you want Russian or Persian (Iranian) caviar?

Wir tranken zuerst einen polnischen dann einen russischen Wodka.
First we drank a Polish, then a Russian vodka.

Sie kaufte viele französische Käsesorten.
She bought many French cheeses.

PITFALL

Adjectives in *-er* derived from the names of cities are capitalized.

Berliner Weiße	**Königsberger Klops**
Nürnberger Lebkuchen	**Würzburger Hofbräu**

Letter Writing

RULE

In letters, all forms of "you," including *du* and *ihr* forms, are capitalized.

Ich hoffe, daß Du Dich nicht wieder erkältest, denn Deine Gesundheit sollte Dir wichtig sein.
I hope you won't catch cold again, since your health ought to be important to you.

Mühe sollt Ihr Euch geben, mit Eurer Arbeit fertig zu werden.
You should see to it that you get your work done.

RULE

The adjective "dear" (with appropriate endings) must be repeated if there is a change in gender or number.

Liebe Rose und lieber Hans!
Dear Rose and Hans,

Lieber Vater und liebe Schwestern!
Dear Father and Sisters,

The same distinction between friendly and formal "you" (see "Pronouns," p. 84) is reflected in letter writing. When writing to friends, "dear" is *lieb-*. In commercial correspondence, *sehr geehrt* is used (see Adjective Endings, p. 3). An exclamation point, not a comma or colon, is used in German. The practice of leaving a space before the exclamation point is now less common than formerly.

German usage in writing addresses differs from American usage as follows:

RULE

1. *Straße*, *Allee*, and *Gasse* are usually parts of street names. *Straße* is then abbreviated *-str.*, not *-st.*

Königsallee 23	Bahnhofstr. 12
Glockengasse 4711	Beethovenstr. 69

2. The street is written before the house number. (see above)

3. The *Postleitzahl* ("zip code") precedes the city. Note the following examples of complete addresses:

Deutscher Akademischer Austauschdienst
Kennedyallee 50
D-5300 Bonn-Bad Godesberg
Deutsche Zentrale für Tourismus
Beethovenstr. 69
D-6000 Frankfurt/M.

In international mail, *D* is sometimes prefixed to the *Postleitzahl*. In the case of large cities, the last two digits are 00. They are usually not omitted. With small towns one normally has four digits:

Herrn Heinrich Hartmann
Schumannstr. 18
2800 Bremen

Frau Hella Witte
Bahnhofstr. 1
3094 Bruchhausen-Vilsen

FORMAL LETTERS

Sample salutations

Sehr geehrter Herr!
Sehr geehrtes Fräulein!

Verehrt- is substituted for *geehrt* if one wishes to indicate great respect. *Hochverehrter Herr Professor!* is formal and pompous.

Complimentary closes

Mit freundlichen Grüßen Ihr
Mit besten Empfehlungen verbleiben wir Ihr
Mit vielen Wünschen und Grüßen bin ich Ihr ergebener

Very formal complimentary closes are less frequently found today than formerly:

> Mit dem Ausdruck meiner vorzüglichsten Hochachtung verbleibe ich Ihr Ihnen ergebenster

LETTERS TO FRIENDS

Salutations

Lieber Paul!
Liebe Lotte!
Meine lieben Freunde!
Liebes Kind Anna!

Complimentary Closes

Herzliche Grüße von Deinem Freund
Es grüßt Dich freundlichst Dein
Alles Liebe und Gute wünschen wir Dir
Dir nochmals viele liebe Grüße von Deinem

If you are using the formal *Sie* but want to indicate a degree of cordiality, *lieb* and *sehr geehrt* can be combined.

> Lieber sehr geehrter Herr Müller!
> Liebe sehr geehrte Frau Kranzler!

USEFUL PHRASES FOR LETTER WRITING

Postschließfach (Post Office Box)
Einschreibebrief (Registered letter)
GmbH; e. V. (Incorporated (firms))
Luftpost (Air Mail)
Mit Luftpost (By Air Mail)

The letters in Goethe's *Die Leiden des jungen Werthers,* one of the most famous epistolatory novels ever written, usually express the date by *an* + dative, for example, *am 30. Mai*. Today it is customary to write the place and then express the date by the accusative of definite time.

Hamburg, den 15. Juli 1977
Paris, den 17. April 1978

Division into Syllables

RULE

Compound words are divided according to their parts.

Ansichts-karte   **Eis-schrank**
Recht-fertigung   **Ver-trag**

RULE

Words with single consonants between vowels in simple words are divided before the consonant.

---

ge-hen   **Rei-fe**
bie-gen   **Kra-gen**

RULE

Similar consonants occurring between vowels in simple words are divided between the two consonants.

Dog-ge   **Git-ter**
bren-nen   **Bul-le**

RULE

Dissimilar consonants occurring between vowels in simple words are divided before the last consonant.

---

stin-ken	**Gar-ten**
Tul-pe	**Verwand-ten**

PITFALL

The combination *st* is not divided in simple words. If, however, the *s* of *st* is part of a compound word and the *t* belongs to another part, *st* is divided.

Simple words

ra-sten	**näch-stens**
Fen-ster	**er-stens**

Compound words

Liebes-traum	**Glas-topf**
Donners-tag	**Haus-tür**

PITFALL

The same consonant can appear three times in a German word only if another consonant follows. If three similar consonants appear between vowels, one of the three consonants is dropped.

Consonant following

Fett + Tropfen	**Fetttropfen** (drop of fat)
Sauerstoff + Flasche	**Sauerstoffflasche** (bottle of oxygen)

Between vowels

Schiff + Fahrt	**Schiffahrt** (navigation, shipping)
Stamm + Mutter	**Stammutter** (ancestress)
Still + Leben	**Stilleben** (still life)

Note: When dividing into syllables, however, the three consonants are retained:

Schiff-fahrt	**Still-leben**
Stamm-mutter	**Bett-tuch**

SPECIAL AIDS

10 ■ Numbers, Measurements, Time Expressions

Cardinal Numbers

With the exception of *eins* (see Articles: *Der-* and *Ein-* Words, p. 24) cardinal numbers (*eins, zwei, drei, vier, fünf*, etc.) are not inflected (that is, they have no endings) except in a few specialized uses noted below.

RULE

Eins before a noun is inflected and the *-s* is dropped.

Sie hat ihm einen Apfel gegeben.
She gave him one (an) apple.

In the preceding example *einen Apfel* could be translated as either "one apple" or "an apple." There is no way to distinguish between these two meanings in writing. In spoken German, however, if *einen* were stressed it would mean "one," not "a(n)."

RULE

The *-s* of *eins* is dropped before *einundzwanzig, einunddreißig*, etc. But 101, 201, 301, 1001, etc., retain it:

---

hunderteins, zweihunderteins, dreihunderteins, tausendundeins

---

RULE

Used as a pronoun, *ein* is declined like *dieser*.

Einer der Studenten hat mir geschrieben.
One of the students wrote me.

Eines (Eins) der Mädchen hat eines (eins) seiner Lieder
    gesungen.
One of the girls sang one of her songs.

PITFALL

Zwei and *drei* can have genitive forms in *-er*. It is, however, more common and more colloquial to use *von* and an uninflected cardinal number.

Das ist die Ansicht zweier Ärzte. *or* Das ist die Ansicht von zwei
    Ärzten.
That is the opinion of two doctors.

Er ist der Vater dreier Kinder. *or* Er ist der Vater von drei Kindern.
He is the father of three children.

To avoid confusion between *zwei* and *drei, zwo* is used for "two" on the telephone and sometimes in official language. Analagously, but superfluously, the ordinal *der zwote* is also used by Germans, although there is no similarity of sound between *der zweite* and *der dritte* (the second and the third).

RULE

The cardinal numbers 2–6 can have a rather literary dative plural in *-en*, usually after the preposition *zu*.

---

ein Walzer zu zweien
a waltz together (for two)

Ich bin die Ruhe zwischen zweien Tönen (Rilke) .
I am the rest between two notes

RULE

Sech-, not *sechs* (6), is used to form *sechzehn* (16) and *sechzig* (60). *Sieb-,* not *sieben,* is used in *siebzehn* (17) and *siebzig* (70).

RULE

German numbers 21–29, 31–39, etc., follow the pattern of the English nursery rhyme "four and twenty blackbirds." They are written as one word.

Thus *vierunddreißig* is 34 (four and thirty) and not 43 *(dreiundvierzig).*

The German mystic tradition (Meister Eckhart, Jakob Böhme, Angelus Silesius, etc.) is significant but those interested in number mysticism would find it difficult if they had to write out numbers such as *achttausendachthundertachtundachtzig* (8,888). Fortunately, you won't often see such mammoth words since they are usually written numerically.

RULE

Masculine and neuter nouns of weight, measure, or value are not used in the plural when preceded by a cardinal number.

Mark (the monetary unit) is the only feminine noun which is treated similarly. In the following examples, note that English "of" is not expressed by either the genitive or *von*.

Wir tranken fünf Glas Bier.
We drank five glasses of beer.

Sie kaufte drei Pfund Bananen und zwei Sack Kartoffeln.
She bought three pounds of bananas and two sacks of potatoes.

Mit dreißig Mark kommen wir nicht aus.
We can't get along with (on) thirty Marks.

Diese Tomaten sehen gut aus. Geben Sie mir bitte sechs Stück!
These tomatoes look nice. Give me six of them please.

Die Dame im Film verzehrte täglich vier Dutzend Eier.
The lady in the movie ate four dozen eggs daily. (English usage resembles German in this example.)

Seine Frau hat fünfzig Paar Schuhe.
His wife has fifty pairs of shoes.

Arithmetical Operations

The four arithmetical operations are expressed in German as follows:

Addition:

$7 + 7 = 14$ **sieben und sieben ist vierzehn** *or*
sieben plus sieben gleich vierzehn

Subtraction:

$11 - 3 = 8$ **elf weniger drei ist acht** *or*
elf minus drei gleich acht

Multiplication:

$3 \times 3 = 9$ **drei mal drei ist (gleich) neun**

A dot is more commonly used in German to indicate multiplication than an $\times$.

$3 \cdot 3 = 9$

Division:

$12 : 3 = 4$ **zwölf durch drei gleich vier**

Arithmetical operations are often difficult. The *Hexeneinmaleins* (witches' multiplication table) in Goethe's *Faust* is more fun:

> **Du mußt verstehn!**
> **Aus Eins mach Zehn,**
> **Und Zwei laß gehn,**
> **Und Drei mach gleich,**
> **So bist du reich.**
> **Verlier die Vier!**
> **Aus Fünf und Sechs,**
> **So sagt die Hex',**
> **Mach Sieben und Acht,**
> **So ist's vollbracht:**
> **Und Neun ist Eins,**
> **Und Zehn ist keins.**
> **Das ist das Hexen-Einmaleins.**

Ordinal Numbers

The designations cardinal and ordinal numbers are a little confusing. Cardinal numbers and ecclesiastical dignitaries derive their name from the

Latin *cardo* (hinge, turning point). Cardinal numbers are the basic ones which give no information about the number. Ordinals refer to a specific number in a series and answer the question, "Which one?"

RULE

Ordinals are formed by adding *-te* to the numbers 2—19 and *-ste* from 20 on. "First," "third," "seventh," and "eighth" are irregular.

---

der, die, das   erste (the first)
                     zweite (the second)
                     dritte (the third)
                     vierte (the fourth)
                     fünfte (the fifth)
                     sechste (the sixth)
                  *siebte (the seventh)
                     achte (the eighth)
                     neunte (the ninth), etc.

*The older, regular form, *siebente,* is still seen occasionally.

Ordinal numbers are treated like any other adjective and can thus have endings. *Null* (zero) also has an ordinal or adjectival form. A symphony of Anton Bruckner is called *Die Nullte* or *Symphony Number Zero* in English since it was published after the others and since his ninth, the last, was not completed.

RULE

A period is used to abbreviate an ordinal number.

The definite article "the" is omitted in written titles but is used orally. Be careful to supply one when needed.

Elisabeth II., Königin von England (Elisabeth die Zweite)
Elizabeth II, Queen of England

Wilhelm II., letzter Kaiser von Deutschland (Wilhelm der Zweite)
William II, last emperor of Germany

Die Persönlichkeit Friedrichs II. (Friedrichs des Zweiten) . . .
The personality of Frederick II . . .

ein Geschenk von Philipp II. an Rubens (Philipp dem Zweiten)
a gift from Philip II to Rubens

Fractions

RULE

Except for "half," fractions end in *-tel*, which is derived from *Teil* (part). All fractions are neuter and can form compound nouns.

Zwei Herzen in Dreivierteltakt
two hearts in ¾ time

Er verlangte die Bezahlung von zwei Dritteln der Rechnung.
He demanded payment of two-thirds of the bill.

RULE

English uses "half" as a noun, adjective, or adverb. German distinguishes between *die Hälfte* (noun) and *halb* which is used as an adjective, an adverb, or infrequently a noun. When *halb* is used adverbially it, like all adverbs, has no ending.

Noun

Die Hälfte der Studenten demonstrierte, als wir in Heidelberg ankamen.
Half the students were demonstrating when we arrived in Heidelberg.

Ich habe nur die Hälfte davon gegessen.
I only ate half of it.

Tristan verlangte die Hälfte des Tranks.
Tristan asked for half the drink.

Ein Viertel ist weniger als ein Halb.
A quarter is less than a half.

Adjective

Sie kaufte ein halbes Dutzend Eier.
She bought a half dozen eggs.

Das Baby aß nur eine halbe Banane; der Affe eine ganze.
The baby ate only half a banana; the monkey a whole one.

Er ist mit halber Geschwindigkeit gefahren.
He drove at half speed.

Adverb

Das Geschäft war schon halb ausgeplündert, als die Polizei ankam.
The store was already half plundered (looted) when the police arrived.

Sie erzählte alles nur halb.
She just told half the story.

The Metric System *(Das Dezimalsystem)*

German-speaking areas of Europe use the metric system. If you are in school now, or are a scientist, this system poses no problems or pitfalls for you, as the metric system is now widely taught in U.S. schools and plans call for its general adoption.

Measurements *(Maßbezeichnungen)*

1. *Linear Measures (Längenmaße)*   Approximate U.S. Equivalent

   1 Zentimeter = 10 Millimeter   0.3937 inches

   1 Meter = 100 Zentimeter   39.37 inches or
   1.094 yards

   1 Kilometer = 1000 Meter   0.6214 mile

2. *Square Measures (Flächenmaße* or *Quadratmaße)*

   1 Quadratzentimeter   0.155 square inch

   1 Quadratmeter   10.764 feet

   1 Quadratkilometer   247.1 acres or
   0.3861 square mile

   1 Hektar   2.47 acres

3. *Measure of Capacity (Hohlmaße)*

   1 Liter   1.057 quarts or
   .264 gallon

4. *Weights (**Gewichte**)*

1 Gramm	.035 ounces
1 Kilogramm	2.2046 pounds

A simple, approximate way to convert kilometers to miles is to multiply the number of kilometers by six and omit the last digit. Thus, 70 kilometers are approximately 42 miles.

PITFALL

A German *Meile* is not an American "mile." *Meile* is not widely used and means "league." Similarly, *Pfund* (pound) is heavier than the American pound.

German Pfund	500 grams
American pound	454 grams

Add or subtract ten percent to convert weights from one system to the other. If, for example, a boxer weighs *zweihundert Pfund* in Germany, he would weigh 220 pounds on an American scale. An American who weighs 120 pounds might be pleased to find that she weighs only 108 *Pfund* in Germany.

Telling Time

To ask, "What time is it?" the following are used:

Wieviel Uhr ist es?
Wie spät ist es?

You should have no trouble with the following:

Es ist 3 Uhr.
It is 3 o'clock.

Es ist Viertel nach drei.
It is a quarter past (after) three

Es ist Viertel vor neun.
It is a quarter of (to) nine.

PITFALL

Um halb vier does not mean "at 4:30" but "at 3:30." English refers to the hour just completed, but German thinks of the hour coming up. Thus *halb* means half the way to the hour expressed.

Wir sind um halb zwei eingeschlafen.
We fell asleep at 1:30.

Ich bin um halb neun aufgestanden.
I got up at 8:30.

Kommt doch mal zu uns, nachmittags um halb vier, sagten Mae und Marlene.
Come up and see us sometime, afternoons at 3:30, said Mae and Marlene.

Viertel can also be used in this way, but this usage is less common. Thus 10:45 can be expressed as *dreiviertel elf* (three quarters of the way to 11:00). *Viertel vor elf* (a quarter to eleven) or *zehn Uhr fünfundvierzig* (10:45) are more common, and easier for students.

PITFALL

The preposition *um* means "at" when telling time, not "around."

Wir sind um 11 Uhr nach Hause gekommen.
We got home at 11.

Er fährt morgen um acht (Uhr).
He leaves tomorrow at eight (o'clock).

To express "around" or "about," in the sense of "approximately," use *ungefähr* or *gegen.*

Wir kamen ungefähr um 3 Uhr an.
We arrived around 3 o'clock.

Komm morgen gegen 6 (Uhr).
Come tomorrow about 6 (o'clock).

German *Uhr*, like English "o'clock," can be omitted from the sentence. When *Uhr* is omitted, *eins* must be substituted for *ein.*

Er kommt um ein Uhr. *or* **Er kommt um eins.**
He's coming at one o'clock. He's coming at one.

THE 24-HOUR CLOCK

Timetables and official announcements use the 24-hour clock. Thus 1:00 PM becomes *13 Uhr,* 2:00 PM becomes *14 Uhr,* and so on. For "midnight" *vierundzwanzig Uhr* or *null Uhr* is used; a theatrical performance is scheduled to finish *gegen 24:00 Uhr,* but a plane leaves at 0.17 (*null Uhr siebzehn*).

If you are talking about when your train, ship, or plane leaves, it is customary to use the 24-hour clock.

Mein Zug fährt um 19 Uhr.
My train leaves at 7:00.

Otherwise, conversational usage is as in English.

Wir haben um 7 Uhr gegessen.
We ate at 7 o'clock.

Time Expressions

> RULE
>
> The accusative is used for definite time, the genitive for indefinite time.

Definite time

Er blieb nur einen Tag.
He stayed for only one day.

Sie verbrachte drei Jahre in Berlin.
She spent three years in Berlin.

Wir haben den ganzen Tag gearbeitet.
We worked all day.

Indefinite time

Eines schönen Tages wird er kommen, dachte Butterfly.
One fine day he'll come, thought Butterfly.

Eines Morgens, als er spazieren ging . . .
One morning as he went walking . . .

Note: The feminine noun *Nacht* forms, by analogy, a genitive of indefinite time with the -*s* endings associated with the masculine and neuter genitive.

Eines Nachts ist er fortgegangen.
One night he went away.

PITFALL

In time expressions the prepositions "on," "at," "in," "for," and "since" pose special problems.

1. *An* + dative (contracted to *am*) is used to express "on" or "in" before days and parts of the day.

Am Dienstag ist er wieder zurück.
On Tuesday he'll be back.

Am 20. Juli fand das Attentat statt.
On July 20 the assassination attempt took place.

Am Abend haben wir getanzt.
In the evening we danced

Exception: in der Nacht (in the night, at night)

2. **In** + dative is used before the months and the seasons, and before *Augenblick, Minute, Woche, Monat, Periode, Jahr, Jahrhundert, Zeit, Zeitalter, Epoche,* and *Ära.*

Im Juni haben sie geheiratet.
In June they got married.

Im Sommer fahren wir nach Europa.
We're traveling to Europe in the summer.

Im Augenblick ist nichts zu machen.
At the moment nothing can be done.

Note the following idiom:

heute in acht Tagen }
heute über acht Tage } a week from today

3. **Um** means "at," not "around," when telling time.

Um 8 Uhr beginnt die Vorstellung.
The performance begins at 8 o'clock.

4. **Zu** is used before *Weihnachten, Neujahr, Ostern,* and *Pfingsten* to express "at" or "for," although it can be omitted idiomatically.

(Zu) Weihnachten war die ganze Familie beisammen.
The whole family was together for Christmas.

(Zu) Ostern hat sie sich ein neues Kleid gekauft.
She bought herself a new dress for Easter.

5. "For" is expressed by **auf** or **für** but these words are frequently omitted.

Sie waren zwei Wochen in Kalifornien.
They were in California for two weeks.

Er hat drei Jahre in Europa studiert.
He studied in Europe for three years.

6. **Seit**, not **für**, is used for a period of time beginning in the past and extending into the present. (See "Verbs," p. 102.)

Wir sind schon seit einem Monat hier.
We have already been here for a month.

Er geht schon seit einem Jahr in die Schule.
He's been going to school for a year already.

Ich arbeite seit Jahren in der Fabrik.
I've been working in the factory for years.

In time expressions, *an, in,* and *vor* always take the dative.

Am Abend haben wir Karten gespielt.
In the evening we played cards.

Sie ist im Oktober angekommen.
She arrived in October.

Vor 35 Jahren wohnten sie in Königsberg.
They lived in Königsberg 35 years ago.

RULE

Sich amüsieren is used for "to have a good time." Never use *eine gute Zeit haben.*

Wir haben uns im Sommer sehr gut amüsiert.
We had a very good time in the summer.

RULE

In time expressions, *erst* is translated as "only" or "just."

Sie ist erst neun Jahre alt.
She is only nine years old.

Laß mich in Ruhe! Ich bin erst angekommen.
Leave me alone. I just got here.

RULE

Never use *Zeit* in multiplication or in expressions for "how many times." *Zeit* is a general word for "time." *Mal* is a specific word.

Zwei mal zwei ist vier.
$2 \times 2 = 4$

zum ersten Mal	**zum dritten Mal**
for the first time	for the third time
zum zweiten Mal	**zum letzten Mal**
for the second time	for the last time
einmal	
once, one time	
zweimal	
twice, two times	

Dates

To ask: "What's today's date?" the following are used:

Der wievielte ist heute?
Den wievielten haben wir heute?
Welches Datum ist heute?

PITFALL

English and German usage differ in the writing and abbreviation of dates.

English:	August 6, 1939	8/6/39
	October 31, 1932	10/31/32
German:	**der 6. August 1939**	6.8.39
	der 31. Oktober 1932	31.10.32

Note: In writing letters the place is given first, then the date. The accusative of definite time, *den,* is used.

New York, den 5. Januar *or* **New York, den 5.1.**

RULE

In is not used alone before years. One must say either *im Jahre 1914* or use the numerical designation alone.

Der Krieg ist im Jahre 1914 ausgebrochen.
The war broke out in the year 1914.

Der Krieg ist 1914 ausgebrochen.
The war broke out in 1914.

Schiller ist im Jahre 1805 gestorben.
Schiller died in the year 1805.

Schiller ist 1805 gestorben.
Schiller died in 1805.

11 ■ Pronunciation

German Long Vowels, Diphthongs, Long Umlauted Vowels		Approximate English Equivalents
Long Vowels:	a	palm, heart, art, God
	e	straight, gay, way, chaos
	ı or ie	fleet, martini, police
	o	row, boat, Ohm, rose
	u	gloom, doom, bloom, sure
Diphthongs:	au	flower, power, bowels
	ei or ai	my, fine, wine, Kaiser
	eu or äu	anoint, royal, oil
Long Umlauted Vowels:	ä	able, hail, grail
	ö	first, bird, curd (pronounced with the lips forward and strongly rounded)
	ü	sweet, dream, gleam (long German *i* + lips rounded)

German Short Vowels and Um- lauted Vowels		Approximate English Equivalents
	a	frond, pond
	e	wed, bed, head

i	bitter, lilt, twig
o	up, butter, offensive, done, of
u	full, bull
ä	den, glen, men
ö	earl, herb (German short *e* + lips rounded)
ü	in, sin, gin (German short *i* + lips rounded)

Be careful not to slur or drawl German vowels. They are more precisely articulated than English vowels, especially in the pronunciation of American English. The dull vowel sound *uh* is also frequent in English, as in *rough, up, mother,* and two of the three "*a*'s" in *banana.* The *-berg* and *-burg* of *Heidelberg* and *Hamburg* are two different, distinct sounds in German. Yet speakers of English often pronounce them with the same dull "*uh*" sound. This probably accounts for the frequent mispronunciation and misspelling of the famed German city *Nürnberg,* which in English is written *Nuremberg* (not *-burg*).

There are no silent vowels or diphthongs in German. Vowels (and consonants) pose far fewer problems for the student than in English where silent letters and pronunciation inconsistencies abound. Once you have learned German pronunciation, you can relax, for there are very few deviations.

German vowels are long when they are:

1. followed by a single consonant
2. followed by an *h*
3. doubled

Long	*Short*
fühlen	füllen
Mut	Mutter
Hüte	Hütte
stören	störrisch
Öl	Hölle
kam	Kamm
Bahn	Bann
Beet	Bett
Ton	Tonne

wohnen	Wonne
Sohn	Sonne
Vater	Vatti
fahren	fallen
wen	wenn
den	denn

Problems in Pronunciation

ei, ie   German *ei* is always pronounced as in English *height*.
German *ie* is always pronounced as in English *priest* or *thief*.

Eis (ice)	Wiese (meadow)
Preis (price)	niesen (to sneeze)
bleiben (to remain)	blieb (remained)
weinen (to cry)	Wiesel (weasle)

b, d, g   These consonants pose no problem except at the end of a word or preceding a consonant when they are pronounced, respectively, *p*, *t*, *k*. Contrast the following examples; those on the left are pronounced as in English, whereas those on the right are pronounced *p*, *t*, *k*.

lieben	liebt, liebte
leben	lebt, lebte
glauben	glaubt, glaubte
Hände	Hand
Freunde	Freund
Hunde	Hund
Ende	endlich
lügen	Lügner
Wagen	Wagner
genügen	genug

ch   The German front *ch*, as in *ich*, and the back *ch*, as in *Bach*, are difficult for students. A good way to learn them is to practice panting like a dog. *Whisky*, *human*, and *hew* should be repeated, emphasizing the *h* sound.

chs   When followed by an *s*, *ch* is pronounced like a *k*.

wachsen	sechs
nächste Woche	Sachsen

Otherwise, avoid the *k* sound when pronouncing *ch*.

h   Never say *hen* in words like the following:

gehen	**stehen**
sehen	**wehen**

If you have studied French or Spanish, you know that *h* is silent in those languages. It is also not pronounced in some English words, for example, *hour, herb, honest,* etc. German *h* is always pronounced before a vowel. When it follows a vowel it is silent and serves to lengthen that vowel. This is true of the above examples and of words like the following:

Fehler	**Mähren**
Ohm	**stehlen**

th   Today many words formerly spelled with a *th* are spelled simply with a *t*. *Th* for *t* may still be encountered in older books. The older spelling *Rathskeller* is familiar to Americans as a kind of pub. Names like *Blumenthal, Rosenthal,* and *Rothschild* are fixed. If they were coined today, they would not have an *h* since the word for valley or dale is now spelled *Tal,* and the word for red is *rot*. In words like *Theater* and *Theorie* (mainly of Greek origin) where *th* still occurs, it is pronounced as a *t*. Thus Germans have great difficulty with the English *th* sound and pronounce it either *s* or *d*.

sch, sh   The sound *sh* as in *shut* is always written *sch* in German, except for initial *sp* and *st* (see below).

Bischof	**Schwert**
Schwein	**Schlummer**
Schmalz	**Ischtar** (Babylonian fertility goddess)

Sch is never separated in German. Do not pronounce the German *sh* like English *shower* or *shave*. The German title of Walt Whitman's *Leaves of Grass* is *Grashalme,* a composite of *Gras* and *Halme,* each pronounced separately. It is similarly wrong to mispronounce *bisher* (till now) as if it were the nonexistent *bischer*. The two components, *bis* and *her* are sounded separately.

sp, st   When they begin a word or syllable, *st* and *sp* are pronounced *scht* and *schp*, as in *spielen, spitzen, stoßen, Stein*. When a connecting *s* is used to link a noun beginning with *t* or *p*, do not say *scht* or *schp*. Liszt's *Liebestraum* and the *Liebestod* from Wagner's *Tristan und Isolde* are compounds of *Lieb* + *Traum* or *Tod* connected by an *s* sounded as a voiceless *s*.

s   The consonant *s* can be voiced or unvoiced. *Voiced* means that the vocal chords are vibrating. Contrast the following:

Voiced	*Unvoiced*
fuzz	fuss
buzz	bus
houses	house
lousy	louse
carouse	mouse

In German, *s* is always voiced before vowels:

Rose	sagen
Hose	lesen
sanft	genesen
Silber	rasen

But *s* is always voiceless in the following cases:

1. before consonants:
   Sklave, gehst, hast, geniest

2. at the end of a word:
   Glas, Haus, las, genas

ss, ß   The two sibilants *ss* and *ß* have the same sound. Both are always pronounced like an unvoiced *s*. Between two short vowels, it is written *ss*, elsewhere, *ß*. Thus the *ss* in *esse* and the *ß* in *aß*, in *müssen* and *mußten* are pronounced the same way.

kn   The *k* is always sounded in the combination *kn*.

Knabe (boy)	knabbern (nibble)
Knecht (slave; farm-hand)	Knie (knee)
Knackwurst (knockwurst (sausage))	
	knusprig (crunchy)

Knochen (bone)   **Knirps** (dwarf, twerp)

Note: Related to *Knabe* and *Knecht* are the English words *knave* and *knight*, but because of linguistic *slide* or *Bedeutungswandel*, the meanings have changed considerably.

| qu | German *qu* is pronounced *kv*. |

Quantität (quantity)   **Qual** (torment)
Quarz (quartz)   **qualifizieren** (to qualify)
Quelle (source)   **Qualm** (dense smoke; fumes)
Quart (quarto (Typ.))   **Quartier** (quarters, billet)

ng   German *ng* is always sounded as in English *ringer*, never as in English *finger*. Thus the German words *Hunger* and *Finger* do not sound the same as the English words *hunger* and *finger*, although the meanings are the same.

r   German *r* may be tongue-trilled or uvular. Both are permissible, although the uvular *r* is preferable. The tongue-trilled *r* is more common in Austria and Bavaria, and will be easier for you to pronounce than the uvular *r*. To practice the tongue-trilled *r*, vibrate the tip of your tongue up and down rapidly.

v   German *v* is pronounced like English *f*.

vier   **bevor**
Vater   **Volkswagen**

Note: In words of non-Germanic origin *v* is pronounced like English *v*.

Violine   **Vitamin**
November   **Villa**

w   German *w* is always pronounced like English *v*.

Wunderbar! Wotans Weg, Wienerwald
Nirwana, Wischnu, Schiwa, Weltenwalter
Wollen wir jetzt weiter wandern?
Winterstürme wichen dem Wonnemond.

The last example is from Wagner's *Die Walküre* (The Valkyrie).

z, tz German *z* and *tz* are pronounced like *ts* in English *hats, pits, Tsar,* or like the *zz* in *pizza*. *Zarathustras Zeit, Zeus.*

Stress

There are no accent marks in German to indicate what syllable is stressed. Umlauts are not stress or accent marks but indications of a change in sound. It is a characteristic of Germanic languages, like English and German, to stress the first syllable of a word. English stresses the first syllable of most words, even those of non-Germanic origin. German is more conservative and generally retains the original Greek, Latin, or French stress. In the following examples, note that German stresses the last syllable, whereas English stresses the first.

Distanz	brutal	Musik
Eleganz	total	Student

RULE

The inseparable prefixes *be-*, *emp-*, *ent-*, *er-*, *ver-*, *zer-*, are never stressed. (See Verbs, p. 116).

Words taken from French are usually pronounced as in French, i.e., nasals and other features are retained.

Bankier	Arrangement	Restaurant	Genie
Bonbon	Niveau	Café	Abonnement

Umlauts

An umlaut indicates a change in sound. Do not use umlauts indiscriminately in written German. There are a few tricky uses, for example, *nervous* is *nervös* but *nervousness* is *Nervosität; drucken* is *to print, drücken to press, kranken to be sick, kränken to insult; erträglich* and *beträchtlich* but *fraglich.*

RULE
Umlauts are used to form some noun plurals such as:

Vater (father)	Väter (fathers)
Bruder (brother)	Brüder (brothers)

RULE

Umlauts are also used in the feminine forms of many nouns, such as the following members of the canine family:

Wolf (wolf)	**Wölfin** (she-wolf)
Fuchs (fox)	**Füchsin** (vixen)
Hund (dog)	**Hündin** (bitch)

RULE

When the diminutives *-chen* or *-lein* are added, the noun is usually umlauted:

Hund (dog)	**Hündchen** (doggie, puppy)
Vater (father)	**Väterchen** (daddy)
Mutter (mother)	**Mütterchen** (little old lady)

PITFALL

Remember that an umlaut can occur only over *a, o, u,* and *au.* In the case of the latter, be careful to place the umlaut over the *a,* not the *u,* for example, *Häuser, Mäuse, Träume.*

12 ■ Vocabulary Building, Confusions, Regional Variations

Germanic and non-Germanic Vocabulary Contrasted

English is basically a Germanic language, although the two main sources of English vocabulary are both Germanic and Latin (usually through French). Chaucer's poems are full of "yokes" or pairs of words, half Saxon, half Norman French. Authors like James Joyce have frequently used or tried to revive Saxon (German) words in English. In English, one often has a choice between the Germanic or the Latinate word, for example, one may use the more vivid "Lady Luck" or the Latinate "Dame Fortune." Edgar Bergen relates that when, as a young man, he heard the word "ventriloquist" for the first time, he didn't know what it meant, and had to look it up. A German would have had no problem with *Bauchredner*, literally, "belly-talker." A great many medical and scientific words are easy in German but difficult in English because of their Greek or Latin origin. Unless you are up on your medical and scientific studies, you probably will not immediately recognize many of the following English words.

Blutdruckmesser
   (sphygmomanometer)
schielend (strabismal)
Gliederfüßler (arthropoda)
Huftier (ungulate)
Kriechtier (reptile)
Säugetier (mammal)
Beuteltier (marsupial)
Hohltier (coelenterate)
Stinktier (skunk)
Fünflinge (quintuplets)
Viereck (quadrangle, square)

Mitesser (comedo)
Selbstmord (suicide)
Vatermord (parricide)
Harnleiter (ureter)
Mittelmeer (Mediterranean)
Verdauungsstörung (indigestion)
Fingersprache (dactylology)
Wiederkäuer (ruminant)
Tausendfüßler (centipede)–
   the "footage" of this crea-
   ture is remarkably
   greater in German

German students have less of a problem than English-speaking ones in learning that *Hohltiere* "coelenterates" (sea anemones, jellyfishes, etc.) have an enteric cavity which occupies the whole interior of their body. English "hollow" and German *hohl* are related to Greek *koilos*, but not many are aware of this. German *hohl* (hollow) is an ordinary, everyday word, as is *Tier* (animal). Similarly, the German *Huftier* makes it easy to remember that the ungulates are hoofed animals (horses, elephants, etc.). The common German words *kriechen* (to crawl, creep), *saugen* (to suck—the Latin *mamma* from which English "mammal" is derived means "breast"), *Beutel* (pouch—kangaroos and other marsupials have pouches), and *kauen* (to chew) give a much more vivid picture of the animals in the above list than do the Latin and Greek terms used in English. *Stinktier* needs no explanation. English "arthropoda" is Greek whereas "centipede" is Latin-derived. German, in both words, expands the basic notion of "foot," (*Fuß*). Latin- and Greek-derived terms exist in German, too, for example, both *Sauerstoff* and *Oxygen* mean "oxygen," and both *Wasserstoff* and *Hydrogen* mean "hydrogen." Quantities of Latin and Greek terms in German can result in an affected and pompous style. Therefore most scholars are careful not to use them excessively.

To expand your German vocabulary you must remember that German usually develops its own basic words to form abstract concepts and expand meanings. German thereby uses its own resources without having recourse to Latinate terms. *Leben,* for example, can appear in many words:

Nouns

Lebenslauf (curriculum vitae)	**Lebenskraft** (vitality)
Lebenslust (vivacity)	**Lebensreife** (maturity)

A great many more compound nouns, such as *Lebensfrische, Lebensdrang,* etc., are possible.

Verbs

ableben (to die, expire)	**beleben** (to animate)
erleben (to experience)	**verleben** (to spend time)
sich ausleben (to live it up)	**sich einleben** (get settled, adjust)
aufleben (to perk up)	**überleben** (survive)

Adjectives and Adverbs

lebendig (alive, lively)	**lebhaft** (vivacious)
lebensfähig (viable)	**lebensvoll** (vigorous)

Often in English the basic verb is Germanic but compounds are Latinate. This is not usually the case in German, as the following shows:

kommen (to come)	**dazwischenkommen** (intervene)
brechen (to break)	**unterbrechen** (interrupt)
halten (to hold)	**behalten** (to retain, keep)
leben (to live)	**überleben** (to survive)
sprechen (to speak)	**widersprechen** (to contradict)

German Words in English

Since English and German are both members of the Germanic family of languages, you have a head start in German vocabulary. For example, you should have no trouble recognizing *Bring mir meine Schuhe, Die Hand hat fünf Finger, Das Wetter ist kalt*, etc. Many German words are used in English, including *Wunderkind, Gesundheit, Wanderlust, Dachshund, Volkswagen, Zeitgeist, Glockenspiel, Realpolitik, Weltanschauung, Schmalz, Wanderjahre, Weltschmerz,* and *Gemütlichkeit*. Sometimes German words are anglicized and given a variety of spellings, for example, *Kaffeeklatsch*.

"Art" or concert songs are called *lieder* internationally. Other German musical terms used in English are *Sprechstimme, Singspiel, Leitmotif,* and *Liederkranz* (the last word means "choral society" and a cheese created in the U.S.). You may be familiar with good things to eat and drink such as *Wiener Schnitzel, Apfelstrudel, Nürnberger Lebkuchen, Braunschweiger Leberwurst, Salzburger Mozartkugeln, Kasseler Rippchen, Sachertorte, Schwarzwälder Kirschwasser,* and the champagnes *Henkell Trocken* and *Fürst Metternich*.

Because of early German work in psychology, such as Edward von Hartmann's *Die Philosophie des Unbewußten* (1869), and the work of Freud, Jung, Adler, Reich, etc., many German words are used in that field. *Angst* is an everyday German word that means "fear" (less literary than *Furcht*), but when used in English it refers to "anxiety," "existential malaise." *Gestalt* means "shape" or "form" as in Goethe's *Erlkönig, Ich liebe dich, mich reizt deine schöne Gestalt,* but in psychoanalytic terms it denotes configurations or patterns of physical or biological events. *Schrei* "shriek," "scream" and *Angstschrei* are also found. Besides *Psychoanalyse,* Freud occasionally used *Seelenkunde* or *Seelenforschung,* which are German equivalents of the Greek (compare Goethe's use of *Seelenwanderung* for "metempsychosis").

The Second Sound Shift

The Second or High German Sound Shift (about 700 A.D.) resulted in various changes in German pronunciation. The following list points out some of them and should enable you to figure out the meaning of many German words. There are complicated philological aspects to this sound shift that will not be discussed here, but an awareness of the relationships between many English and German words should be of great help in vocabulary building.

German *b* sometimes corresponds to English *f* or *v:*

Abend (evening)   geben (to give)
Dieb (thief)   schieben (to shove)
Diebe (thieves)   streben (to strive)
Leben (life)   leben (to live)
Liebe (love)   halb (half)
Silber (silver)   übel (evil)

German *ch* is often *gh* or *k* in English:

Buch (book)   Woche (week)
Fracht (freight)   weich (weak)
Licht (light)   acht (eight)
Milch (milk)   brechen (to break)
Nacht (night)   machen (to make)
Tochter (daughter)   suchen (to seek)
lachen (to laugh)   kochen (to cook)

German *d* is frequently English *th:*

Ding (thing)   Norden (north)
Dorn (thorn)   dünn (thin)
Durst (thirst)   danken (to thank)
Leder (leather)   denken (to think)

German *ff, pf,* and *f* are frequently *p* in English:

Affe (ape)   Pflanze (plant)
Apfel (apple)   Pfennig (penny)
Kupfer (copper)   pflücken (to pluck)
Pfad (path)   offen (open)
Schaf (sheep)   reif (ripe)

German *g* often corresponds to English *y* or *i:*

Auge (eye)   fliegen (to fly)
Garn (yarn)   legen (to lay)

Nagel (nail)	**liegen** and **lügen** (to lie)
Regen (rain)	**sagen** (to say)
Weg (way)	**gelb** (yellow)
Tag (day)	**gestern** (yesterday)
Note suffix *-ig:*	
lausig (lousy)	**blutig** (bloody)
rosig (rosy)	**heilig** (holy)

German *k* may be *ch, c,* or *k* in English:

keusch (chaste)	**König** (king)
Kirsche (cherry)	**Kuh** (cow)
Katze (cat)	**Köchin** (cook (female))
Kleider (clothes)	**Kalk** (chalk (lime))

German *s, ss,* and *(t)z* often correspond to English *t:*

Fuß (foot)	**Zunge** (tongue)
Faß (vat)	**zahm** (tame)
Haß (hate)	**zehn** (ten)
Schweiß (sweat)	**beißen** (to bite)
Wasser (water)	**essen** (to eat)
Herz (heart)	**setzen** (to set)
Pelz (pelt, fur)	**sitzen** (to sit)

German *sch* is frequently *s* in English:

Schlaf (sleep)	**schnarchen** (to snore)
Schnee (snow)	**schwimmen** (to swim)
Schwert (sword)	**schwingen** (to swing)
schlau (sly)	**schwören** (to swear)
schlachten (to slaughter)	**schwellen** (to swell)

German *t* is often English *d:*

Bart (beard)	**Schatten** (shadow)
Bett (bed)	**Schulter** (shoulder)
Blut (blood)	**Schwert** (sword)
Brot (bread)	**Traum** (dream)
Gott (God)	**waten** (to wade)
Garten (garden)	**hart** (hard)

Etymology and philology are interesting, specialized fields which you may care to investigate on your own. Many English and German words are related but have changed in meaning, for example, *Knabe* (boy) is cognate to "knave," and *sterben* (to die) is related to "to starve." The name of President Hoover's ancestors probably was "Huber." German *Weber* has sometimes been changed to "Weaver," although both names are common in America. Many German names have been Anglicized, for example, Schmidt to Smith, Becker to Baker, Müller to Miller, etc. The family names of Generals Custer and Pershing were originally Küster and Pforschin

German *r* is sometimes English *s* (rhotacism), for example, *Hase* (hare), *Eisen* (iron). Sometimes German *ei* is English *o*, for example, *Seife* (soap), *Heim* (home), *heiß* (hot), *beide* (both). There are many other linguistic processes and phenomena which indicate a variety of relationships between German and English. However, these are beyond the scope of this book.

If you have to look up a word repeatedly and find that you cannot remember it, put a dot next to it each time you look it up in the vocabulary list. When you have accumulated several dots, write the word on a separate sheet and try writing sentences. You may recall similar advice given when learning English: "Use a new word twice and it's yours."

More advanced students should not look up every word but should read for the general context or gist. If you are an intermediate or advanced student, you will improve your vocabulary if you read works in German with which you are already familiar in English. If your recollection of the Grimm *Fairy Tales* has not faded too much, read them in German. If you are very familiar with the Bible in English, get one in German. Hesse's *Steppenwolf* and *Demian* are internationally popular with young people. If you've read Hesse or other authors, such as Kafka or Mann in English translations, read the same works in German. Listening to vocal music and following the text is another good way to improve vocabulary.

Words Frequently Confused

As most people who work with language know, words can wear masks and contain subterfuges. Since English and German are cousins with varying degrees of similarity and dissimilarity, the masks and subterfuges are sometimes more complex. The following words may cause you problems because of slight differences in spelling and/or pronunciation:

das **Ostern** (Easter)

die **Aster** (aster)

die **Auster** (oyster)

das **Australien** (Australia)

das **Österreich** (Austria)

der	Ast (branch)	der	Vogel Strauß (ostrich)
das	Lied (song)	das	Leid (sorrow)
das	Gelächter (laughter)	das	Gelichter (rabble)
	schon (already)		schön (beautiful)
	sehen (to see)		zehn (ten)
der	Nachttisch (night table)	der	Nachtisch (dessert)
	wer (who)		wir (we)
der	Dreck (dirt)	der	Druck (print)
	dann (then)		denn (for; than)
	leben (to live)		lieben (to love)

Definitions of Frequently Confused Words

The following list of words frequently confused is by no means complete but represents a sampling of the errors likely to be made by students. Many other words frequently confused are treated elsewhere in this book.

Nouns are capitalized and gender has been indicated by *m., f., n.*

Akt *m.* This word does not translate as English *act* (**Tat**) except when referring to a stage work. **Akt** means *nude model* (painting and sculpture) and *legal document.* **Akten** are *official files;* **Aktien** are *stocks* or *shares.* **Aktion** is more comprehensive than English *action* (**Handlung**), and often translates as *activity* or *drive,* as in **Wohltätigkeitsaktion,** *charity drive.*

aktuell This word means *up-to-date* or *timely,* not *actual.*

Allee *f.* This is not an *alley* (**Gasse**) but an *avenue* or *thoroughfare* usually lined with trees or statues. The **Königsallee** in Düsseldorf and the **Siegesallee** in Berlin are imposing streets.

also This does not mean *also* (**auch**) but *thus* or *therefore.* Nietzsche's *Also Sprach Zarathustra* means *Thus Spoke Zarathustra.*

Anger *m.* This word means *meadow,* not *anger* (**Zorn**).

Art *f.* This does not mean *art* (**Kunst**) but *manner, way, type.* A student once incorrectly translated *Martern aller Arten* from Mozart's *Entführung* as "Martin (Jack) of all trades." It means "Tortures of all kinds."

Artist *m.* This does not mean *artist* (**Künstler**) but *circus or nightclub performer.*

Asyl *n.* This word is not used for a *lunatic asylum* (**Irrenanstalt**). It means *sanctuary* or *refuge.*

ausnehmen   This word means *to take out* only in the sense of *to exempt* or *to eviscerate.*

Bad *n.*   This means *bath*, not *bad* (böse, schlecht). Many German spas (Bad Pyrmont, etc.) are beautiful places.

bald   This means *soon.* The English word *bald* is kahl.

Beere *f.*   This means *berry*, not *beer.*

bekommen   This word means *to get* or *obtain*, not *to become* (werden). The conductor Bruno Walter once said, in a radio interview, "I became my first job . . ." when he meant "I got my first job."

beten   Forms of this weak verb (beten, betete, gebetet) which means *to pray* should not be confused with the strong verbs *to ask* (bitten, bat, gebeten) and *to offer* (bieten, bot, geboten). A more bizarre confusion is with the strong verb *to bite* (beißen, biß, gebissen).

(For a discussion of weak and strong verbs, see chapter on Verbs, p. 100. See also Tables of Principal Parts, p. 142.)

Bier *n.*   This means *beer*, not *coffin stand* (Bahre).

brav   German has taken only one of the two French meanings, *well-behaved* or *decent*, not *brave.*

Brief *m.*   This does not mean *brief* (kurz) but a *letter.*

Brüder *m.*   This means *brothers* in general. **Gebrüder** should be used only for names of firms. Thus it is wrong to refer to the Grimm brothers as the **Gebrüder Grimm** unless they are in business together.

Chef *m.*   English has taken only the meaning *chef de cuisine* (chief cook) from the French. German uses it more generally to mean the head of a firm, department, etc.

Dose *f.*   This means *box* or *tin can. Dose* (medicine) is **Dosis.**

Fabrik *f.*   This means *factory. Fabric* is **Gewebe.**

famos   This does not mean *famous* (berühmt) but *splendid* or *terrific.*

fast   This means *almost* or *nearly*, not *fast* (schnell). To *fast* is fasten, whereas *to fasten* is **befestigen, anbinden.**

feist   This means *plump* or *fat.* A *feist* is a small dog in American English, and *feisty* means *spunky* or *frisky*, concepts not generally associated with fat. German **satt** means *full* or *satiated.*

Fleisch *n.*   This word is used for both *meat* and *flesh*.

fort   This means *away* or *off*. *Fort* is **Festung, Burg** or even **Fort**. A *ford* (river) is a **Furt** and *Furze* (botany) is **Ginster**.

Frauenzimmer *n.*   This is an archaism used humorously or disparagingly to refer to a female. It does not mean the *ladies' room* (**Damentoilette**).

Gang *m.*   This does not mean *gang* (**Bande**) but *motion, course,* or *corridor*.

geistig   This means *pertaining to the mind, spirit, culture,* whereas **geistlich** means *clerical, pertaining to things ecclesiastic*. **Geist** is a *spirit* or *ghost*. **Gespenst** is a *spook*.

genial   A **geniales Werk** is not a *genial work,* but *a work which shows genius*.

Gift *n.*   This means *poison,* not *gift* (**Geschenk, Gabe**). **Mitgift**, however, is a *dowry*.

Gymnasium *n.*   In German, a **Gymnasium** is a pre-university secondary school. *Gym* is **Turnhalle**.

hold   This does not mean *to hold* (**halten**) but *graceful, charming,* or *lovely*.

kindisch   This means *childish,* whereas **kindlich** means *childlike*.

Kirche *f.*   This means *church*. **Kirsche** is *cherry*.

Kissen *n.*   This means *pillow*. **Küssen** is *to kiss*.

Kitsch *m.*   This word has nothing to do with *kitchen* (**Küche**). It refers to art objects in questionable taste.

klappen   This means *to flap* or *strike together*. Most frequently, however, it means *to work out well, click*. **Alles klappte gut** means *Everything went off well*. **Klappe** means *lid* or *trap*. The expression **zwei Fliegen mit einer Klappe schlagen** means *to kill two birds with one stone*. **Beifall klatschen** means *to applaud*.

kontrollieren   In addition to *to control,* this word also means *to check* or *inspect*.

Lachen *n.*   This is a verbal noun meaning *laughter*. Do not confuse it with **die Lache**, which means *pool* or *puddle*.

Last *f.*   This means *load* or *burden*. *To last* is **dauern; währen**. A *shoemaker's last* is **Leisten**.

Leier *f.* This means *lyre* (Music). A *liar* is **Lügner.**

List *f.* This means *cunning.* **Verzeichnis, Liste** mean *list.*

Lust *f.* This rarely means *lust* (**Sinnenlust**). Its basic meaning is *pleasure* or *delight.*

Made *f.* German **Made** means *maggot.* The English "Made in Germany," is used internationally in commerce.

Mann *m.* This means *male being* or *man.* In reference to mankind in general, **der Mensch** is used.

Mist *m.* This does not mean *mist* (**Nebel**) but *manure* or *dung.*

Neuigkeit *f.* This means *news* or *something new.* **Neuheit** is *a new design* or *creation* in fashion (*haute couture*). **Neuerung** is an *innovation.*

niederkommen This means *to be confined, lie in* (pregnancy), not *to come down.*

phantasieren In addition to *to fantasize,* this also means *to improvise.* (Music)

raffiniert This means *refined* only in an industrial sense (sugar, oil, etc.). When applied to people it means *cunning* or *crafty.*

Rasen *m.* This means *lawn* or *turf.* **Rasen** is the verb meaning *to rage* or *rave.* **Rasieren** is a verb meaning *to shave; raze.* Germans sometimes confuse **rasend** (raving) with **rasant,** a military term used to describe a flat trajectory.

Rat. *m.* This means *counsel* or *advice,* not *rat* (**Ratte**). A **-rat** is also a *councillor* and the word was attached to many civil service ranks. **Medizinalrat** is still used in the GDR. **Das Rad,** pronounced similarly to **Rat** (See Pronunciation), means *wheel.*

sächsisch This does not mean *sexy* but *Saxon.*

Sekt *m.* This does not mean a *religious sect* (**die Sekte**) or an *insect* (**das Insekt**) but *champagne.* **Champagner** is also used but the proper and now most frequently used word for non-French champagne is **Sekt.**

spendieren This does not mean *to spend* (**verbringen, ausgeben**) although spending is involved in its meaning, *to buy something for someone* or *to give a treat.*

tasten This does not mean *to taste* (**schmecken, kosten**) but *to touch* or *handle.*

Tod *m.*   This is the noun meaning *death*, as in Schubert's *Der Tod und das Mädchen.* Do not pronounce it like the name *Todd.* The adjective **tot** (same pronunciation as **Tod**) means *dead.* **Töten** is *to kill;* **sterben**, *to die.* The unrelated verb *to tote* is **schleppen**.

toll   This means *crazy* or *mad.* The English word *toll* is **Zoll** (tariff) and **Glockengeläute** (bells).

weiß   This means *white. Wise* is **weise**. **Viese** is a *meadow* and **Waise** is an *orphan.* The noun **Weise** means *way, manner; tune.* This latter meaning is found in Sarasate's *Zigeunerweisen.*

Wien *n.*   This means *Vienna.* **Wein** is *wine. Wien und der Wein* is a popular Viennese *Heurigen* song. "Heurig" is related to **heute**; it refers to the Viennese custom of drinking local wines very soon after they are ready.

Particles

The following words, called *particles, fillers,* or *expletives,* have a variety of idiomatic translations. Mastery of them will come only after long exposure to the German language. It is possible to have a highly idiomatic sentence filled with these words. The simple *Was ist los?* can become the following:

Was ist ja doch denn auch nur los?
I wonder whatever in the world can possibly be the matter

aber   In addition to its basic meaning, *aber* has many idiomatic uses. It is often used for emphasis.

Das war aber schön!
That was really beautiful!

Aber nein!
Not at all!

auch   In addition to "also" *auch* can mean "even" or "either":

Die sind auch froh darüber.
They're even glad about it.

Das wird ihnen auch nichts nützen.
That won't do them any good either.

Auch can also confirm, correct, or reinforce:

Sie ist schön und hilfsbereit. Das ist sie auch.
She's beautiful and ready to help. She is that indeed *or* She certainly
is.

Das wollen wir auch tun.
We certainly do intend to do that.

denn   In addition to the conjunction "for" (See Conjunctions, p. 40),
denn can be used as a filler to reinforce meaning:

Was ist denn los?
What can be the matter?

doch   Besides meaning "nevertheless," "anyway," "after all," *doch* inten-
sifies an imperative and contradicts a question to which one expects a
negative answer:

Er war doch ein guter Mensch, sagte die Witwe.
After all (nevertheless) he was a good man, said the widow.

Hol mir doch meine Pfeife!
Go and get my pipe, will you?

Du gehst heute nicht ins Kino, nicht wahr?—Doch!
You're not going to the movies tonight, are you? "Yes I am!"

ja   This word has a wide range of idiomatic meanings:

Das ist ja unerhört!
That's outrageous!

Da kommt ja mein Freund.
There he comes, my friend.

Steigen Sie ja dort nicht aus!
Whatever you do, don't get off there.

Es gehen ja Mühlenräder in jedem klaren Bach. (W. Müller)
After all millwheels turn in every clear brook.

nur   In addition to the meaning "only," *nur* can also intensify:

Tun Sie das so schnell wie nur möglich!
Do that as quickly as possible.

Die sollen nur kommen!
Just let them come!

schon   Besides "already," *schon* can mean "even" or "only." It is also very
idiomatic and must often be omitted or paraphrased:

Geh schon!
Go. (Go on now. Get going.)

Ich werde es schon schaffen.
Don't worry, I'll get it done.

Schon am nächsten Tag verließ er sie.
The (very) next day, he left her.

More Confusing Words

Many of the following words are homonyms (words that sound alike but have different meanings) in English. Pay attention to dictionary markings; meanings which diverge are set off by a semicolon. Nouns are capitalized and gender has been indicated by *m., f., n.*

to ask   **fragen** (a question); **bitten um** (for something)

band   **Kapelle** *f.* (music); **Band** *n.* (ribbon); **Binde** *f.* (bandage); **Bande** *f.* (gang)

bank   **Bank** *f.* (money); **Ufer** *n.* (shore)

bark   **Rinde** *f.* (tree); **Bellen** (canine)

beam   **Balken** *m.* (construction); **Strahl** *m.* (optics)

bishop   **Bischof** *m.* (ecclesiastic); **Läufer** *m.* (chess)

blade   **Blatt** *n.* (grass, paper); **Klinge** *f.* (razor)

board   **Ausschuß** *m.* (committee); **Brett** *n.* (lumber); **Kost** *f.* (food); **Kost und Logis** (room and board)

bone   **Knochen** *m.* (mammals); **Gräte** *f.* (fish); **Bein** ("leg" and sometimes in general)

bow   **Bogen** *m.* (weapon); **Bug** *m.* (nautical); **Verbeugung** (curtsy)

butt   **Stummel** *m.* (cigarette); **Arsch** *m.* (behind); **Zielscheibe** (target)

capital   **Hauptstadt** *f.* (city); **Kapital** *n.* (finance); **Großbuchstabe** *m.*, **Majuskel** *f.* (typography)

case   **Kiste** *f.* (container); **Fall** *m.* (law, event)

chance   **Gelegenheit** *f.* (opportunity); **Zufall** (accident)

club   **Keule** *f.* (instrument); **Verein** *m.* (association)

date   **Dattel** *f.* (fruit); **Verabredung** *f.* (appointment); **Datum** *n.* (calendar) *diet* Kost, Nahrung, Diät *f.* (culinary); Tag *m.* (political assembly) as in Landtag, Reichstag

drive Fahrt *f.* (in a vehicle); Trieb *m.* (psychology)

economy Wirtschaft *f.* (science); Sparsamkeit *f.* (thrift)

fortune Glück *n.* (luck); Reichtum *m.* (wealth); Zufall *m.* (chance)

gag Jux *m.* (prank); Witz *m.* (witticism); Knebel *m.* (muzzle)

glasses Gläser *f.* (drinking); Brille *f.* (eye)

key Schlüssel *m.* (door); Taste *f.* (typewriter, piano, etc.); Tonart *f.* (music)

lap Schoß *m.* (human frame); Runde *f.* (sports)

letter Brief *m.* (communication); Buchstabe *m.* (alphabet)

to lie lügen (falsehood); liegen (recline, be recumbent). *Note:* legen (to lay) is the causative of liegen. The confusion occurs primarily in English because the past tense of *to lie* is *lay*.

to live leben (in general); wohnen (reside). Lebensraum means *living space* (a political concept) not *living room* (Wohnzimmer)

lock Schloß *n.* (door, etc.); Schleuse *f.* (canal); Locke *f.* (hair). The verb locken means *to lure*, not *to lock* (schließen)

mole Maulwurf *m.* (animal); Muttermal *n.* (birthmark)

papers Papiere *n.* (in general); Ausweis *m.* (identification); Zeitungen *f.* (newspapers)

pipe Rohr *n.* (conduit); Pfeife *f.* (smoking)

plain Ebene *f.* (topography); einfach (simple)

plane Flugzeug *n.* (airplane); Hobel *m.* (tool)

play Spiel *n.* (game); Schauspiel, Drama *n.* (theater)

record Schallplatte *f.* (music, disc); Höchstleistung *f.* (sports); Aufzeichnung, Urkunde *f.* (documentation)

rest Ruhe *f.* (repose); Rest *m.* (leftover)

royalty Königswürde *f.*, Adel *m.* (nobility); Tantieme *f.* (from books)

rule Regel, Vorschrift *f.* (conduct); Herrschaft *f.* (government)

save sparen (thrift); schonen (to spare); retten (life, souls)

scale Waage *f.* (weight); Schuppe *f.* (fish); Tonleiter *f.* (music)

sentence Satz *m.* (grammar); Urteil *n.*, Rechtsspruch *m.* (law) *sheet*   Bettuch, Bettlaken *n.* (bed); Blatt *n.* (paper)

to spend   verbringen (time); ausgeben (money)

spring   Frühling *m.* (season); Feder *f.* (mechanical)

suit   Anzug *m.* (clothing); Prozeß, Rechtshandel *m.* (law)

swallow   Schluck *m.* (liquids); Schwalbe *f.* (bird)

tank   Behälter *m.* (container); Panzer *m.* (military)

volume   Band *m.* (book); Inhalt *m.* (cubic capacity)

wait   To *wait for* is warten auf with the accusative. *He waits for her* is Er
wartet auf sie. Er bedient sie means *He waits on her* in the sense
that he serves her (dinner, etc.). Bedienen (compare Dienst, *service)*
also has the specialized meaning *to follow suit* in card playing. Ewar-
ten means *to expect* and *to wait impatiently,* when it is often used with
können and kaum as in Ich kann sie kaum erwarten/die erste
Blum im Garten (Goethe's *Der Musensohn).* Abwarten means *to
wait patiently* or *to wait and see.* The noun *weight* is Gewicht *n.* and
the verb *to weight* is belasten or beschweren (literally, *to make
heavy).* A *waiter* (restaurant) is Kellner *m.*

wake   Kielwasser *n.* (nautical); Begräbnisfeier *f.* (funeral)

wife   Frau is most frequently used. Gemahlin and Gattin are stilted
(spouse). Weib is sometimes used for *wife* but more often refers to
woman in a general sense.

will   Wille *m.* (volition); Testament *n.* (legacy)

work   Arbeit *f.* (job); Werk *n.* (literary or artistic)

writer   Schreiber *m.* (letter, clerk); Schriftsteller *m.* (professional);
Dichter *m.* (poetry, literature)

Regional Variations

German is spoken not only in Germany but in many other areas of
Europe as well. Austria, Liechtenstein, the greater part of Switzerland, and
Luxemburg are German-speaking. France, Belgium, Denmark, Italy, and
many areas of Eastern Europe have German-speaking minorities. Within
Germany itself there is considerable dialectical diversity. Verbs such as
schwäbeln, berlinern, sächseln, etc., describe the speech characteristic of
those areas (Swabia, Berlin, Saxony). *Böhmeln* refers to the German spoken
in Bohemia (now part of Czechoslovakia).

Regional writers *(Heimatdichter)* like Groth, Reuter, Hebel, and Rosegger, are well represented in German literature. Of course they write deliberately in their local dialect. Occasionally authors who write standard German use localisms. Schiller, aware of the Swabian predilection for the incorrect and indiscriminate use of *ver-*, wrote *zerschiedene Edelsteine*, although *verschiedene Edelsteine* is correct. Goethe, in *Faust*, rhymes *neige* and *Schmerzenreiche* because of his Frankfurt dialect. Some authors mix dialect and standard German *(Schriftdeutsch)* in the same work to characterize individuals, for example, Bavarian in Wedekind's *Der Marquis von Keith* and Silesian in Hauptmann's *Vor Sonnenaufgang*.

The regional and the local have played an important role in German history ever since the days when the map of Germany was a mosaic of kingdoms, principalities, duchies, bishoprics, etc. The dialect diversity between North and South is often accompanied by personality caricatures. The Northerner is often described as businesslike, efficient, and snappy *(schneidig* and *schnodderig)*, in contrast to the easy-going Southerner *(Gemütlichkeit, Schlamperei, Lederhosen,* "oom-pah-pah," etc.). Austrians and Southerners delight in opposing the "harsh Prussian" with the *gemütlich* Austrian. *Ja ja, der Wein is' guot (gut), i (ch) brauch ka' neien (neuen) Huot (Hut), i (ch) setz mein' alten auf, bevor i (ch) a (ein) Wasser sauf . . .* goes a Viennese *Heurigen* wine song.

Anyone who has spent any time in Germany will quickly note the diversities in German speech. In the South the *r* is trilled on the tip of the tongue. In the North, the uvular *r* is used. In Hannover many people don't pronounce *sp* and *st (stoßen auf einen spitzen Stein) schp* and *scht* where they should (initially), and many Southerners always pronounce them *schp* and *scht* even where they should not *(erst, Fenster)*. As the refrain goes, *In Berlin und auch an der Wieden* (i.e., in Vienna), *da spricht man Deutsch, aber es klingt verschieden*.

Southerners rarely use the imperfect (past) tense or the imperfect subjunctive (Subjunctive II). Even greetings differ: In the South one usually hears *Grüß Gott* for *Guten Tag*, and *gelt?* (a dialect form of *gilt es?*) for *nicht wahr? Tag* is often pronounced *Tach* in the North. *Tschüß* (corruption of French *adieu*) is heard in the North. *Auf Wiederschauen* is more popular than *Auf Wiedersehen* in Austria. North and South also differ in the use of the auxiliaries *sein* and *haben* in the perfect tenses. The quality of vowels and intonational patterns are also quite different. A joke has it that a North German thought his Bavarian friend had mastered Chinese after the two had spent only one day in China, as the Bavarian awakened him with the words *Wach auf. Die Sonn' scheint schon lang*, pronounced in the Bavaria. dialect. Southerners omit the vowel *e* whenever they can. One hears *Schulz* and *Kraus* in the South, but *Schulze* and *Krause* in the North. The optional dative *e* on some nouns (*zu Hause*) is also more common in the North. Umlauted forms are less popular in Bavaria and Austria and are frequently incorrectly omitted in the spoken language (*du fährst, er läßt*, etc.). *Brücke* (bridge) is written with an umlaut in standard German. But the Austrian city *Innsbruck* has none, whereas northern cities like *Osnabrück* have an umlaut. Generally, the further north one goes, the more umlauts occur. Many culinary terms for the same dish vary. For example, North and South are united in their love of real whipped cream; however, Austrians do not say *Schlagsahne*, but *Schlagobers*.

LOW GERMAN

Low German or *Plattdeutsch* is still spoken in Northern Germany. *Platt* means *flat* and aptly describes the terrain of Northern Germany. High German or *Hochdeutsch* is historically associated with the mountainous South. Many people, including Germans, sometimes misuse the term *High German* when referring to standard German. A better word is *Schriftdeutsch*, i.e., spoken German which does not deviate from written German.

Some words are used only in Low German areas, for example, *knif*, not *Messer*, for "knife." Often, both High and Low German words exist side-by-side, for example, *Brunnen* and *Born, feist* and *fett, sanft* and *sachte, sühnen* and *versöhnen, Waffen* and *Wappen*. North Germans generally speak Standard German more carefully, omitting fewer letters, than Southerners, because the North's Low German is very different from the High German which developed in the South. The Second or High German Sound Shift did not touch Low German. A park in Hamburg is called *Planten un Blomen*, not *Pflanzen und Blumen*. Low German is in many respects similar to English. The following Low German poem by Theodor Storm illustrates this point.

> *Low German:*   Gode Nacht
> Över de stillen Straten
> Geit klar de Klokkenslag;
> God Nacht! Din Hart will slapen,
> Un morgen is ok en Dag.

High German: Gute Nacht
Über die stillen Straßen
Geht klar der Glockenschlag;
Gute Nacht! Dein Herz will schlafen,
Und morgen ist auch ein Tag.

Another North German poet, Klaus Groth, declared in a famous little poem *Schlicht un Recht* (Simple and Right), that whether it was High or Low (German), dry or wet, beer or wine, rough or fine, it had to be genuine.

Hoch oder platt	Hoch oder platt
Drög oder natt	Trocken oder naß
Beer oder Win	Bier oder Wein
Grof oder fin	Grob oder fein
Awer echt mutt et sien.	Aber echt muß es sein.

Once you have mastered Standard German, you will be able to appreciate the rich store of humor provided by dialects. Saxon, Swiss, and Alsatian parodies of Schiller and others are examples. Vienna supplies quantities of Graf Bobby jokes, Cologne has Tünnes and Schäl, Hamburg has Klein Erna.

Regionalisms reflect uniqueness and individuality. One aim of this book has been to demonstrate the genius of the German language. It is hoped that this aim has been fulfilled.

Bibliography

Apelt, Mary L. and H.-P., *Reading Knowledge in German for Art Historians and Archaeologists,* E. Schmidt Verlag, Berlin, 1975.

Bach, Adolf, *Geschichte der deutschen Sprache,* Quelle & Meyer, Heidelberg, 1965.

Bergethon, K. Roald and Frank X. Braun, *Grammar for Reading German,* Houghton Mifflin Company, Boston, 1963.

Betteridge, Harold T., *The New Cassell's German Dictionary,* Funk and Wagnalls, New York, 1958.

................., *Der Sprach Brockhaus,* Brockhaus, Wiesbaden, 1968.

Curme, G.O., *A Grammar of the German Language,* Macmillan, New York, 1970.

Dornseiff, Franz, *Der deutsche Wortschatz nach Sachgruppen,* De Gruyter, Berlin, 1965.

................., *Der Große Duden. Grammatik,* Dudenverlag des bibliographischen Instituts, Mannheim, 1966.

Eggeling, H.F., *A Dictionary of Modern German Prose Usage,* Clarendon Press, Oxford, 1961.

Farrell, R.B., *Dictionary of German Synonyms,* Cambridge University Press, Cambridge, 1953.

Goedsche, C.R. and Meno Spann, *Deutsch für Amerikaner,* American Book Company, New York, 1960.

Hearn, W.J. and G. Seidmann, *Graded German Composition,* Macmillan, New York, 1966.

Jacobs, Noah J., *Embarrassing Moments in German, and How to Avoid Them,* Frederick Ungar Publishing Co., New York, 1956.

Kelling, Hans-Wilhelm and Marvin Folsom, *Wie man's sagt und schreibt,* Holt, Rinehart and Winston, New York, 1969.

Kluge, Friedrich, *Etymologisches Wörterbuch der deutschen Sprache,* 20th Edition, De Gruyter, Berlin, 1967.

Koelwel, Eduard, *Wegweiser zum richtigen Deutsch*, Langenscheidt, Berlin, 1957.

Küpper, Hans, *Wörterbuch der deutschen Umgangssprache*, Claassen, Hamburg, 1956.

Moulton, W.G., *The Sounds of English and German*, University of Chicago Press, Chicago, 1962.

Priebsch, Robert and W.E. Collinson, *The German Language*, Faber and Faber, London, 1968.

Reiners, Ludwig, *Stilkunst*, C.H. Beck'sche Verlagsbuchhandlung, München, 1961.

Schmitz, F.J., *Learning German*, Appleton-Century-Crofts, New York, 1948.

Siebs, Theodor, *Deutsche Aussprache*, De Gruyter, Berlin, 1960.

Textor, A.M., *Sag es treffender*, Rowohlt, Hamburg, 1968.

Wahrig, Gerhard, *Das große deutsche Wörterbuch*, C. Bertelsmann, Gütersloh, 1967.

Wängler, Hans et al., *Deutsch unserer Zeit*, Holt, Rinehart and Winston, New York, 1969.

Waterman, J.T., *A History of the German Language*, University of Washington Press, Seattle, 1976.

Wildhagen, K. and W. Héraucourt, *The New German Dictionary*, Follett Publishing Company, Chicago, 1965.

Wustmann, Gustav, *Sprachdummheiten*, Edited by Werner Schulze, De Gruyter, Berlin, 1966.

■ Index

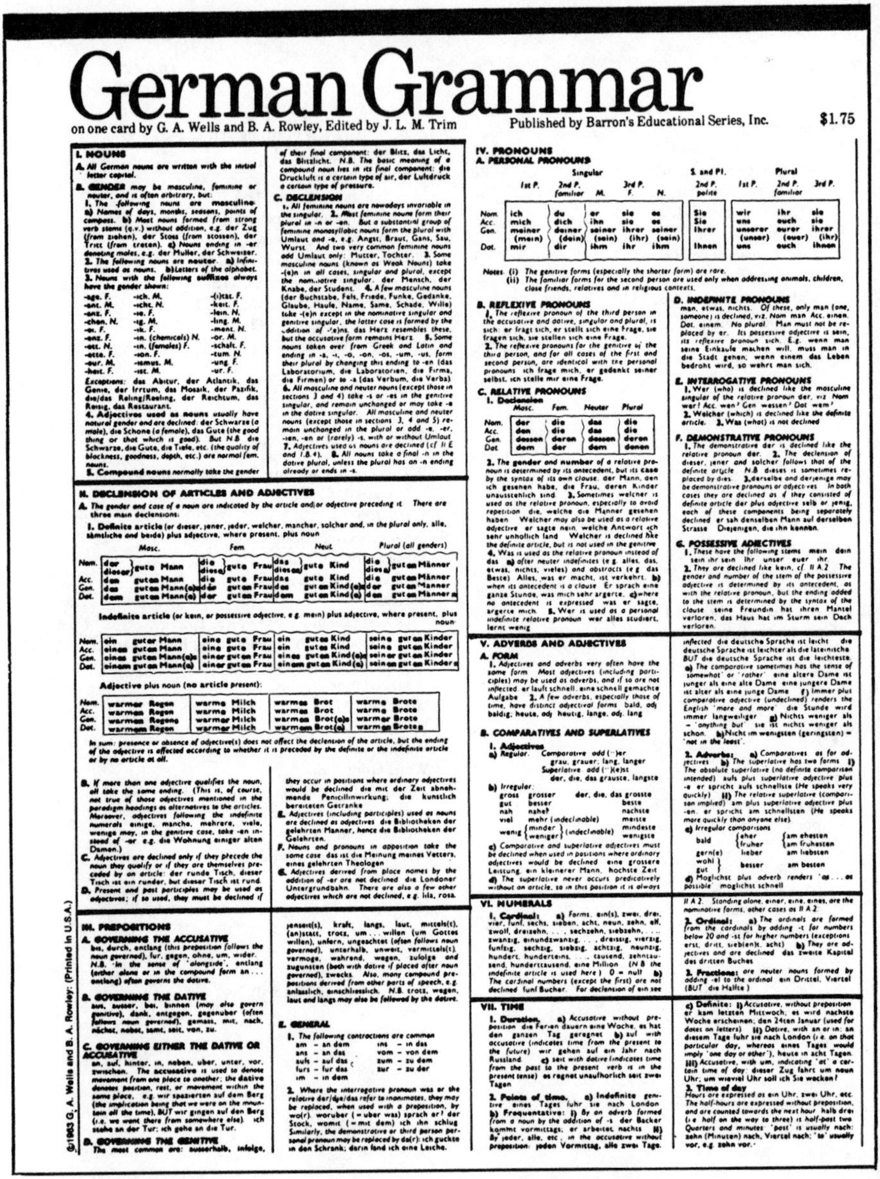

German Grammar

on one card by G. A. Wells and B. A. Rowley, Edited by J. L. M. Trim   Published by Barron's Educational Series, Inc. $1.75

I. NOUNS

A. All German nouns are written with the initial letter capital.

B. GENDER may be masculine, feminine or neuter, and is often arbitrary, but:

1. The following nouns are masculine:
a) Names of days, months, seasons, points of compass. b) Most nouns formed from strong verb stems (q.v.) without addition, e.g. der Zug (from ziehen), der Stoss (from stossen), der Tritt (from treten). c) Nouns ending in -er denoting males, e.g. der Müller, der Schweizer.

2. The following nouns are neuter: a) Infinitives used as nouns. b)Letters of the alphabet.

3. Nouns with the following suffixes always have the gender shown:

-age. F.	-ich. M.	-(s)tat. F.	
-ant. M.	-icht. N.	-keit. F.	
-anz. F.	-ie. F.	-lein. N.	
-chen. N.	-ig. M.	-ling. M.	
-ei. F.	-ik. F.	-ment. N.	
-ent. M.	-in (chemicals) N.	-or. M.	
-enz. F.	-in. (females) F.	-schaft. F.	
-ette. F.	-ion. F.	-tät. F.	
-heit. F.	-ismus. M.	-ung. F.	
-keit. F.	-ist. M.	-ur. F.	

Exceptions: das Abitur, der Atlantik, das Genie, der Irrtum, das Mosaik, der Pazifik, das/der Rating/Reeling, der Reichtum, das Reng, das Restaurant.

4. Adjectives used as nouns usually have natural gender and are declined: der Schwarze (a male), die Gute (the good thing or that which is good). But N.B. das Schwarze, das Gute, die Tiefe, etc. (the quality of blackness, goodness, depth, etc.) are normal fem. nouns.

5. Compound nouns normally take the gender of their final component: der Blitz, das Licht, das Blitzlicht. N.B. The basic meaning of a compound noun lies in its final component: der Druckluft is a certain type of air; der Luftdruck a certain type of pressure.

C. DECLENSION

1. All feminine nouns are nowadays invariable in the singular. **2.** Most feminine nouns form their plural in -n or -en. But a substantial group of feminine monosyllabic nouns form the plural with Umlaut and -e, e.g. Angst, Braut, Gans, Sau, Wurst. And two very common feminine nouns add Umlaut only: Mutter, Tochter. **3.** Some masculine nouns (those of weak Nouns) take -(e)n in all cases, singular and plural, except the nominative singular: der Mensch, der Knabe, der Student. **4.** A few masculine nouns (der Buchstabe, Fels, Friede, Funke, Gedanke, Glaube, Haufe, Name, Same, Schade, Wille) take -(e)n except in the nominative singular and genitive singular, the latter case is formed by the addition of -(e)ns; das Herz resembles these, but the accusative form remains Herz. **5.** Some nouns taken over from Greek and Latin and ending in -a, -i, -o, -on, -os, -um, -us form their plural by changing this ending to -en (das Laboratorium, die Laboratorien, die Firma, die Firmen) or to -a (das Verbum, die Verba). **6.** All masculine and neuter nouns (except those in sections 3 and 4) take -s or -es in the genitive singular, and remain unchanged or may take -e in the dative singular. All masculine and neuter nouns (except those in sections 3, 4 and 5) remain unchanged in the plural or add -e, -er, -en, -en or (rarely) -s with or without Umlaut. **7.** Adjectives used as nouns are declined (cf. I E and I.B.4). **8.** All nouns take a final -n in the dative plural, unless the plural has an -n ending already or ends in -s.

II. DECLENSION OF ARTICLES AND ADJECTIVES

A. The gender and case of a noun is indicated by the article and/or adjective preceding it. There are three main declensions.

1. Definite article (or dieser, jener, jeder, welcher, mancher, solcher and, in the plural only, alle, sämtliche and beide) plus adjective, where present, plus noun

	Masc.	Fem.	Neut.	Plural (all genders)
Nom.	der gute Mann	die gute Frau	das gute Kind	die guten Männer
Acc.	den guten Mann	die gute Frau	das gute Kind	die guten Männer
Gen.	des guten Mann(es)	der guten Frau	des guten Kind(es)	der guten Männer
Dat.	dem guten Mann(e)	der guten Frau	dem guten Kind(e)	den guten Männern

Indefinite article (or kein, or possessive adjective, e.g. mein) plus adjective, where present, plus noun

	Masc.	Fem.	Neut.	Plural
Nom.	ein guter Mann	eine gute Frau	ein gutes Kind	seine guten Kinder
Acc.	einen guten Mann	eine gute Frau	ein gutes Kind	seine guten Kinder
Gen.	eines guten Mann(es)	einer guten Frau	eines guten Kind(es)	seiner guten Kinder
Dat.	einem guten Mann(e)	einer guten Frau	einem guten Kind(e)	seinen guten Kindern

Adjective plus noun (no article present):

	Masc.	Fem.	Neut.	Plural
Nom.	warmer Regen	warme Milch	warmes Brot	warme Brote
Acc.	warmen Regen	warme Milch	warmes Brot	warme Brote
Gen.	warmen Regens	warmer Milch	warmen Brotes	warmer Brote
Dat.	warmem Regen	warmer Milch	warmem Brot	warmen Broten

In sum: presence or absence of adjective(s) does not affect the declension of the article, but the ending of the adjective is affected according to whether it is preceded by the definite or the indefinite article or by no article at all.

B. If more than one adjective qualifies the noun, all take the same ending. (This is, of course, not true of those adjectives mentioned in the paradigm headings as alternatives to the articles. Moreover, adjectives following the underlying numerals mancha, mehrere, viele, wenige may, in the genitive case, take -en instead of -er e.g. die Wohnung weniger alten Damen.)

C. Adjectives are declined only if they precede the noun they qualify or if they are themselves preceded by an article: der runde Tisch, dieser Tisch ist rund, aber dieser Tisch ist rund.

D. Present and past participles may be used as adjectives; if so used, they must be declined as adjectives.

III. PREPOSITIONS

A. GOVERNING THE ACCUSATIVE
bis, durch, entlang (this preposition follows the noun governed), für, gegen, ohne, um, wider. N.B. 'in the sense of 'alongside', 'entlang' (either alone or in the combined form an ... entlang) often governs the dative.

B. GOVERNING THE DATIVE
aus, ausser, bei, binnen (may also govern positive), dank, entgegen, gegenüber (often follows noun governed), gemass, mit, nach, nächst, nebst, samt, seit, von, zu.

C. GOVERNING EITHER THE DATIVE OR ACCUSATIVE
an, auf, hinter, in, neben, über, unter, vor, zwischen. The accusative is used to denote movement from one place to another; the dative denotes position, rest, or movement within the same place, e.g. wir spazierten auf dem Berg (the implication being that we were on the mountain all the time), BUT wir gingen auf den Berg (i.e. we went there from somewhere else). Ich stehe an der Tür; ich gehe an die Tür.

D. GOVERNING THE GENITIVE
The most common are: ausserhalb, infolge,

IV. PRONOUNS

A. PERSONAL PRONOUNS

	Singular						Plural		
	1st P.	2nd P. familiar	3rd P.			S and Pl. 2nd P. polite	1st P.	2nd P. familiar	3rd P.
			M.	F.	N.				
Nom.	ich	du	er	sie	es	Sie	wir	ihr	sie
Acc.	mich	dich	ihn	sie	es	Sie	uns	euch	sie
Gen.	(meiner) (mein)	(deiner) (dein)	seiner (sein)	ihrer (ihr)	seiner (sein)	Ihrer	unser	euer	ihrer
Dat.	mir	dir	ihm	ihr	ihm	Ihnen	uns	euch	ihnen

Notes: (i) The genitive forms (especially the shorter form) are rare.
(ii) The familiar forms for the second person are used only when addressing animals, children, close friends, relatives and in religious contexts.

B. REFLEXIVE PRONOUNS

1. The reflexive pronoun of the third person in the accusative and dative, singular and plural, is sich; er fragt sich, er stellt sich eine Frage, sie tragen sich, sie stellen sich eine Frage. **2.** The reflexive pronouns for the genitive, and the first and second person, are identical with the personal pronouns: ich frage mich, er gedenkt seiner selbst, ich stelle mir eine Frage.

C. RELATIVE PRONOUNS

1. Declension

	Masc.	Fem.	Neuter	Plural
Nom.	der	die	das	die
Acc.	den	die	das	die
Gen.	dessen	deren	dessen	deren
Dat.	dem	der	dem	denen

2. The gender and number of a relative pronoun is determined by its antecedent, but its case by the syntax of its own clause: der Mann, den ich gesehen habe, die Frau, deren Kinder unausstehlich sind. **3.** Sometimes welcher is used as the relative pronoun, especially to avoid repetition die, welche die Männer gesehen haben. Welcher may also be used after an adjective or sagte mein welche Antwort gab sehr unhöflich sind. Welcher is declined like the definite article, but is not used as a relative adjective or sagte mir, welche Antwort gib. **4.** Was is used as the relative pronoun of das alles, etwas (das, welches, vieles) and abstracts (e.g. das Beste) Alles, was er macht, ist verkehrt, bg when an antecedent is a clause. Er sprach eine ganze Stunde, was mich sehr ärgerte, (wherein no antecedent is expressed was or sagte, ärgerte mich. **5.** Wer is used as a personal relative pronoun wer alles studiert, lernt wenig.

D. DEMONSTRATIVE PRONOUNS

1. The demonstrative der is declined like the relative pronoun der. **2.** The declension of dieser, jener and solcher follows that of the definite article. N.B dieses, etwas replaced by dies. 3.derselbe and derjenige may be demonstrative pronouns or adjectives. In both cases they are declined as if they consisted of definite article der plus adjective selb or jenig, each of these components being separately declined as such denselben Mann auf demselben Strasse Diejenigen, die ihn kannten.

E. POSSESSIVE ADJECTIVES

1. These have the following stems: mein (sein tein ihr sein Ihr unser euer ihr. **2.** They are declined like kein, cf. II A.2 The gender and number of the stem of the possessive adjective is determined by its antecedent, as with the relative pronoun, but the ending added to the stem is determined by the syntax of the clause seine Freundin hat ihren Mantel verloren, das Haus hat im Sturm sein Dach verloren.

V. ADVERBS AND ADJECTIVES

A. FORM

1. Adjectives and adverbs very often have the same form. Most adjectives (including participles) may be used as adverbs, and so are not inflected or laufe schnell. anna schnell gemachte Aufgabe. **2.** A few adverbs, especially those of time, have distinct adjectival forms: bald, oft, baldig, heute, oft, heutig, lange, oft, lang.

B. COMPARATIVES AND SUPERLATIVES

1. Adjectives
a) **Regular.** Comparative -er grau, grauer; lang, länger. Superlative -(e)st der, die, das grauste, längste
b) **Irregular:** gross grosser der, die, das grosste gut besser der, die, das beste nah näher nächste viel mehr (indeclinable) mehrste weng (minder) (indeclinable) mindeste **2.** Comparative and superlative adjectives must be declined when used in positions where ordinary adjectives would be declined: eine grössere Leistung, ein kleinerer Mann. höchste Zeit **3.** The superlative never occurs predicatively without an article, so in this position it is always

VI. NUMERALS

1. Cardinal: a) Forms ein(s), zwei, drei, vier, fünf, sechs, sieben, acht, neun, zehn, elf, zwölf, dreizehn ... sechzehn, siebzehn ... zwanzig, einundzwanzig ... dreissig, vierzig, fünfzig, siebzig, achtzig, neunzig, hundert, hunderteins, ... hundertzwei ... senc hundertzwanzig eine Million (N.B the indefinite article is used here's I 0 = null) b) The cardinal numbers (except the first) are not declined fünf Bücher. For declension of ein see

VII. TIME

1. Duration. a) Accusative without preposition die Ferien dauern eine Woche; es hat den ganzen Tag geregnet. The count of accusative (indicates time from the present to the future) wir gehen auf ein Jahr nach Russland. c) seit with dative indicates time from the past to the present: seit drei Tagen, for the present tense) er regnet unaufhörlich seit zwei Tagen **2. Points of time.** a) Indefinite genitive eines Tages (ihr sie nach London kommen, will). b) Frequentative: b) an adverb formed from a noun by the addition of -s der Becker kommt vormittags, er arbeitet nachts **3.** bei jeder, alle, etc., in the accusative without preposition: jeden Vormittag, alle zwei Tage,

(text continued, right-hand columns largely abbreviated grammatical notes)

CARD GUIDE TO GERMAN GRAMMAR

All the fundamentals of grammar at your fingertips—condensed but large enough to be read easily. On a varnished 8½" × 11" card, punched to fit any 3-ring binder. 2-sided, $2.50, Canada $3.50

Barron's Educational Series, Inc., P.O. Box 8040 • 250 Wireless Blvd., Hauppauge, NY 11788
Call Toll-Free: 1-800-645-3476, in NY: 1-800-257-5729
In Canada: Georgetown Book Warehouse, 34 Armstrong Ave. • Georgetown, Ont. L7G 4R9
Call Toll-Free 1-800-668-4336

All prices are in U.S. and Canadian dollars and subject to change without notice. At your bookseller, or order direct adding 10% postage (minimum charge $1.50, Can. $2.00), N.Y. residents add sales tax.